Sometimes
Reading
Is
Hard

Using decoding, vocabulary,
and comprehension strategies
to inspire fluent, passionate,
lifelong readers

ROBIN BRIGHT

Pembroke Publishers Limited

Special Note: Thank you to Stephen Parker, who granted permission for use of the phonics notation system used throughout this book. Parker's notation system first appears in his free ebook, *Reading Instruction and Phonics*, available for download at www.ParkerPhonics.com.

Images on page 147 appear with permission from Scholastic Canada.

© **2021 Pembroke Publishers**
538 Hood Road
Markham, Ontario, Canada L3R 3K9
www.pembrokepublishers.com

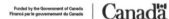

Library and Archives Canada Cataloguing in Publication

Title: Sometimes reading is hard : using decoding, vocabulary, and comprehension strategies to inspire fluent, passionate, lifelong readers / Robin Bright.

Names: Bright, Robin M., author.

Identifiers: Canadiana (print) 20210149515 | Canadiana (ebook) 20210149566 | ISBN 9781551383514 (softcover) | ISBN 9781551389516 (PDF)

Subjects: LCSH: Reading (Elementary)

Classification: LCC LB1573 .B726 2021 | DDC 372.4—dc23

Editor: Margaret Hoogeveen
Cover Design: John Zehethofer
Typesetting: Jay Tee Graphics Ltd.

Printed and bound in Canada
9 8 7 6 5 4 3 2 1

Contents

Introduction: Setting Off Down the Path

Literacy is a bridge from misery to hope. It is ... the road to human progress and the means through which every man, woman and child can realize his or her full potential.
—Kofi Annan, former United Nations' Secretary-General, 1997

Let's talk about reading. Reading is a fundamental skill, crucial for learning and achieving in school and beyond. Worldwide research shows that lack of basic reading skills leads to lack of school achievement, low self-esteem, poor health, poverty, and crime. Simply put, reading is key to economic and social development.

In school, reading is necessary for almost everything students do. A glance into any classroom shows students reading morning messages, posters, anchor charts, timetables, lists, textbooks, labels, worksheets, assignments, syllabi, board work, tests, websites, PowerPoint presentations, and a wide variety of books. Outside of school, students read signs, posters, emails, social media sites, magazines, notes, books, comic books, manuals, song lyrics, catalogues, recipes, and birthday cards.

Not being able to read is like being barred from a members-only club—many aspects of life are off limits.

Many of us take reading for granted. But what if we had never learned that skill? Not being able to read is like being barred from a members-only club—many aspects of life are off limits. Further, illiteracy contributes to feelings of shame and low self-worth, the collateral damage of an inability to read. Teachers and parents see first-hand the pain, frustration, anger, and sadness experienced by students struggling to read. What happens to the student who cannot yet read in Grade 4, when she sees that everyone else can? What happens to her in Grade 6, 8, or 12 if she stays in school that long?

Learning to Read Is Work

Despite the unequivocal value of reading, we have no guarantee that all children will master the skill. Reading, unlike speaking, does not come naturally. It must be learned. "Human beings were never born to read," writes Maryanne Wolf, a Tufts University cognitive neuroscientist and child development expert. Reading is a remarkably complex cognitive process that some have described as a "neurological triple backflip."

The good news is that we know a great deal about how to teach reading. We know that teaching reading involves phonemic awareness and phonics knowledge, fluency, vocabulary, and comprehension (Adams, 1990). We also know that these components of reading are interrelated and work together to build strong and rich reading abilities.

A Responsibility to Break the Cycle

Even when teachers focus students' attention on the reading components and have well-established reading programs, they are challenged every new school year by a new set of students and the unique backgrounds they bring to reading. The teachers I know are eager and diligent. They tell me that they cannot wait to meet and care for a new group of students at the start of every school year—students who will have new and different reading needs. Perhaps there will be a new student unfamiliar with English, another student who says he doesn't like reading, or a student who gets stuck and gives up. Then there are the students who come to school who know how to read but choose not to read.

No matter the student's situation, we have a responsibility to every one of them.

At a public library presentation a few years ago, I was speaking on the topic of how to support reading development in young children at home. The audience was filled with young, hopeful, caring parents eager to help their children become successful, enthusiastic readers. I cannot now recall the details of the presentation. But what happened afterward has stayed with me to this day.

An older gentleman remained in the room after almost everyone had gone. I thought he was probably a grandparent. Perhaps he had a question to ask. He said to me, "Do you know why I came tonight? I came to learn how to break the cycle." He proceeded to tell me that he himself could not read and that his son, a long-distance truck driver, had struggled with reading his entire life. And now, the gentleman told me, he had a grandson.

This grandfather had come to my presentation to learn the secret of learning to read. He told me of his hopes to help his grandson find a new pathway, one different from the pathway he and his son had taken.

Stories like this tell me that we cannot underestimate the value and power of reading and our critical role as teachers in making it happen in our classrooms. We have a duty to teach our students *how* to read and to inspire them to *want* to read.

Every teacher I know believes that reading is a universal right. Ability to read opens doors in the same way that not being able to read closes them. We know this to be true through the experience of our own lives as teachers, parents, caregivers, and citizens. In these roles we read what we need to read to do our jobs, live our lives, act as caregivers, pursue hobbies and interests, travel, stay informed, and do just about anything else we want or need to do.

Learning How to Teach Reading Is Work

I vaguely recall taking a course on reading in my teacher education program. I even tutored a child as part of a practicum. So I wasn't sent into the classroom bereft of tools to teach reading. But the truth is, I really learned how to teach

As teachers, we have a duty to teach our students *how* to read and to inspire them to *want* to read.

reading in my first teaching position as a Grade 1 teacher. And I know I am not the only one. Consider the comments of these two experienced educators.

> I remember when I first got a full-time teaching position at an elementary school. I was replacing an experienced teacher. I remember exactly where I was standing when I asked her, "How do you teach kids to read?" I figured I knew some strategies for helping kids learn to be interested in reading, and I had incentives and strong communication skills up my sleeve. But what I did not know was how to teach them *how* to read.
> —*Linda, school administrator*

> I have to admit, as a classroom teacher, teaching reading and writing was a huge fear of mine! I specifically stayed away from Grade 1 for this reason.
> —*Melanie, school administrator*

You may now be facing the question that virtually all teachers of reading face at one point or another: "How do I teach reading?" Perhaps you are in a new teaching position in Kindergarten or the primary grades. Perhaps you are facing students in elementary or middle school who are uninterested in reading. Perhaps you teach high school, and your students' poor reading skills are affecting their level of achievement in other subjects. Perhaps you are working with students whose first language is not English. Or perhaps this is the year you finally decided to give reading more attention by investing whole-heartedly in professional learning on this invaluable topic.

Even at my most confident as a teacher, I stayed awake at night thinking about my students and how to support and inspire them in their reading. It's possible you do too. The solution is to work at it. Just like reading is a skill that you must work at to master, so is teaching reading. It doesn't just pop out of the air—if you want to reach all your students, you need to develop a large toolbox of skills.

I have no doubt that you will have the power to turn any fears or uncertainty about teaching reading into successes, just like I did.

The Spark for This Book

I remember when the idea for this book took hold. It came, as might be expected, from my work with a school community. I received a phone call from a principal who had recently moved from an elementary school to a middle school. When he arrived at his new school, the first thing he did was to ask his teachers and staff what team goal they could set that would most support their students in the coming years. They all said reading. The teachers, many of whom had been at that school for years, agreed that their students were bright, creative, funny, and thoughtful. At the same time, they knew that many students were held back in their overall school performance because they lacked basic reading skills and the motivation to read.

The principal asked me, could I help? That phone call led to an extraordinary partnership among me, a teacher educator and researcher, the staff and students, and a group of pre-service teachers. Our goal? To support reading throughout the entire school, in all grades and all areas of the curriculum. Our work together convinced me to write a book that would bring to light not only the lessons and insights learned in that school community but also my almost three decades of

I stayed awake at night thinking about my students and how to support and inspire them in their reading. It's possible you do too.

experience working with teachers, researchers, administrators, literacy consultants and coaches, graduate students, and pre-service teachers to help them teach reading and motivate readers.

Through the decades, my experiences have taught me that the school system is vulnerable to quick-and-easy fixes intended to create better readers but that actually waste everybody's time. Few of these expensive fads make a long-term contribution to teachers' knowledge. We all know the value of reading and, of course, we want all our students to be readers. But there are no shortcuts. *Sometimes Reading Is Hard* helps teachers cut through the fads to focus on the foundational knowledge they need to teach reading.

The title for this book came from a Grade 8 student, Sharlene. She said to me, "Sometimes reading is hard, but I'm up for a challenge." In one short sentence, Sharlene articulated the attitude required to make readers and teachers of readers alike. She also captured what this book is about.

What You Will Find in This Book

I was inspired to organize this book by P. David Pearson's words about reading. Here he identifies the roles and relationship of the four components of reading that form the backbone of this book: *decoding, fluency, vocabulary*, and *comprehension*.

> Decoding is important if it is on the pathway to ... fluency.
>
> Fluency is important if it is on the pathway to ... vocabulary.
>
> Vocabulary is important if it is on the pathway to ... comprehension.
>
> Comprehension is important if it is on the pathway to ... critical reasoning and action in the world. (Frey, 2020)

I wanted this book to highlight the synergy between the skills of reading and the factors of motivation that power a lasting love of reading. I observed this synergy at work in my own children as they learned to read. I saw it as my young students accomplished the astonishing feat of translating letters on the page into sounds, words, and stories.

- Chapter 1 is about helping us develop a common understanding of the importance of reading, the importance of *teaching* reading, and the major considerations needed to teach reading.
- In the following four chapters, we explore the four components of reading —decoding, fluency, vocabulary, and comprehension—and how to teach the skills associated with each. Woven throughout are instructional strategies for developing the factors of motivation—confidence, interest, choice, dedication, and collaboration—so that all students can become capable, passionate, lifelong readers.
- Research tells us that teaching the *skills* of reading together with teaching the *reasons* to read are key. So, the final chapter focuses on how to inspire a love of reading to last a lifetime.

I provide instructional strategies, classroom vignettes, teaching tips, resources, and step-by-step guidance all along the way.

As you read, I will invite you to into classrooms to meet teachers and their students who are learning to be proficient and tenacious, even when reading is hard. The people and practices you will encounter are from my own very real experiences working in schools. It was important to me to preserve the authenticity of classroom voices, so all quotations are true to the original speakers. I have, however, taken care not to match names with specific teaching situations to preserve anonymity. Any inaccuracies in the depictions are my own.

A final consideration: Over and over, while writing, I was drawn to Maryanne Wolf's illuminating phrase that we are all involved in teaching what she calls "the story and the science of reading." Teaching reading well to all students must address the science (the reading components) but, crucially, it should never neglect the story—the aspect of reading that connects us and makes us feel.

> **Teaching reading should never neglect the story—the aspect of reading that connects us and makes us feel.**

Are You Ready to Read?

Sometimes Reading Is Hard is, at its core, about understanding how to teach reading to motivate students to want to read. It is a book I wish had been available when I was a classroom teacher. At the time, I wanted guidance that would give me

- **hope** on the days I wasn't sure I knew what I was doing
- **knowledge** that my decisions were based on solid research and practice
- **strategies** to try that I hadn't used or to retry if they hadn't worked for me in the past
- **perspective** through glimpses into real classrooms, so I could see how other teachers teach reading
- **encouragement** to keep going even when it seemed I wasn't making progress
- **confidence** that maybe I was on the right track after all
- **connection**, so that I would know that I wasn't alone

I hope that this book will provide some of that precious guidance to you.

I am excited for you to meet the many talented teachers whose experiences appear in this book as you re-energize your understanding of teaching reading and expand your repertoire of teaching strategies.

Get ready to set the students in your classroom on a pathway toward the proficiency and passion for reading that they will need to live life to the fullest.

1

What Do You Mean I Have to Teach Reading?

> A large fundamental mistake is the assumption that reading is natural to human beings and that it will simply emerge "whole cloth" like language when the child is ready.
> —*Maryanne Wolf*, Reader, Come Home, *2018*

Have you ever had the pleasure of teaching a young person how to drive? I see you smiling there. My husband and I took turns teaching our two daughters how to drive, shouldering the responsibility (and anxiety) together but also sharing the joy in helping them learn a new skill that would lead them toward independence.

New drivers need to have some basic skill knowledge about vehicles and driving to begin the process. This includes knowing the importance of the parts of the car, such as the steering wheel, ignition, gas and brake pedals, headlights, windshield wipers, turn signals, hazard lights, horn, and parking brake. New drivers also need to know the rules of the road.

The real learning, though, takes place once the new drivers start driving. That's when they learn how to adjust the seat, mirrors, and steering wheel to accommodate their position. They figure out how to start the car and put it in gear, how to ease down on the gas pedal, and how to switch instinctively to the brake pedal when needed.

You don't simply get into the car and start driving. But you also do not spend all your time in a classroom learning the parts of the car and the rules of the road. There must be time for real driving practice and lots of it.

Learning to read works the same way, as a combination of acquiring knowledge and practice. And what gets this major snowball rolling? Motivation.

Even before the lessons began, our daughters were motivated—they *wanted* to learn how to drive! As they practiced, they built up their confidence, which contributes to motivation. At first, the new drivers were tentative as they practiced their driving skills, but with practice their confidence grew. Their confidence fed their motivation, which led to more motivation and more practice.

In the beginning, our daughters had to think about every aspect of the driving process. Over time, they developed into skilled drivers able to drive effortlessly and even without considerable deliberate thought. They learned to coordinate the many processes involved in driving until it all became automatic.

That's not the whole story though. My husband and I know that, regardless of how skilled you are at manoeuvring a car, there will be times when you encounter situations that will challenge and test you. So we made sure that our daughters

Children engage with print in a way that involves not just perception and cognition, but the total self that includes motivations, interests, beliefs, and values.
—**Researchers James Hoffman, James Baumann, and Peter Afflerbach, 2014**

become strategic drivers, able to negotiate the unexpected. Like drivers, readers must be strategic. Reading strategies, like the ones in this book, are tools students can use when they encounter text that is challenging.

I will never forget the look of jubilant excitement on our daughters' faces when they each began driving. I am reminded of that when I see children learn to read.

The Whole Is Greater Than the Sum of Its Parts

Beginner readers, like beginner drivers, need to learn both skills and strategies. Experts agree that skilled readers are those who can fluently decode text so effortlessly that reading becomes automatic. Strategic readers can employ effort and deliberation as they encounter difficulties or barriers in a reading.

Those are the skills and strategies. But what of motivation in reading? If we spend all our time on reading skills and strategies, students might not feel the *why* of learning to read. If we always push texts onto students that they must struggle with to decode or make sense of, we are wasting their time and they will become frustrated and lose their confidence as readers. Just as new drivers need time to practice, students need time to practice what I would call "real" reading—the fun stuff.

Real reading is sparked because someone wants to learn something new and gain knowledge. Or they're just interested and enjoying the experience. Curiosity, interest, and enjoyment are motivational factors that must accompany learning to read. Perhaps most important, real reading is about connecting with others and feeling. It's impossible not to identify with Oliver in the picture book, *Where Oliver Fits* by Cale Atkinson. He feels like an outsider until he finds a place where he belongs. A child reading about Oliver will connect. Real reading builds both interest and confidence. Teachers and students need to do a lot of it! More reading means more opportunities for students to further develop their skills and strategies.

Reading, like driving, requires synergy. The synergy happens at the intersection of reading skills, strategies, and factors of motivation because—and this is the important part—"the whole is greater than the sum of its parts." Some teachers describe the synergy as when something "clicks" for the reader, the point when it all comes together and it works.

There is nothing quite as exciting as watching a child read a book like Mem Fox's *Time for Bed* and say, "I read it all by myself," or a teen who tells you that he has never before read a book like *Long Way Down* by Jason Reynolds and asks you, "Does he have other books?" Students deserve to experience the same kind of jubilant excitement of learning to read that my daughters experienced while learning to drive.

There is nothing quite as exciting as watching a child read a book like Mem Fox's *Time for Bed* and say, "I read it all by myself."

In Mackenzie's Classroom: "When Do I Get to Read Real Books?"

Teacher Mackenzie told me a story of working with Jorge, a student in Grade 3 who was not yet reading at the Grade 3 level and appeared to struggle with certain sounds of letters. She was working with Jorge on sound-symbol relationships, particularly digraphs (that is, the /sh/, /f/, and /ch/ sounds).

Mackenzie did what many of us do: She showed a short musical video on digraphs. She then chose a short book with those particular sounds in them, and then, together, the teacher and the student found the words with digraphs in them. Then the student printed the words in three columns depicting each of the digraph sounds (/sh/, /f/, and /ch/). Mackenzie and Jorge read the words aloud together and finally went back to the book to reread the text.

All this sounds like a well-presented guided reading lesson, doesn't it? But, at the end of the 15-minute session, Jorge looked at his teacher and asked, "When do I get to read real books?" While Jorge had dutifully participated in learning the skills he needed to read, his perception that this wasn't the real thing had to be addressed.

How many students are not as courageous as Jorge and don't ask this question? How many don't even imagine there is something more?

Underlying Considerations in Teaching Reading

In 30 years of working in education, I have been privileged to work closely with talented, caring colleagues, teachers, and pre-service teachers. It only made sense to include them in my research and writing. To prepare to write this book, I asked a group of enthusiastic and successful teachers of reading, with years of experience teaching in elementary, middle, and high school as well as at the post-secondary level, to talk with me about what matters in teaching reading.

My group of trusted subject-matter experts exchanged many emails, had long phone calls, and met regularly on video calls to talk about reading. And they never complained. Just the opposite. It was hard to get us all to stop talking about the joys and challenges of teaching reading. After much lively and thoughtful discussion, I was able to narrow down our views about what matters in teaching reading to a list of nine considerations. Have a look at this list. Do these considerations reflect your teaching philosophy about teaching reading? Do they expand your views? Do they challenge your views?

1. Sometimes reading is hard.
2. Structures of language support reading instruction.
3. The components of reading need to be taught daily.
4. Every teacher is a reading teacher.
5. Meaningful relationships are key.
6. Students need good reasons to read.
7. Teachers must be readers.
8. Reading engagement leads to the goal: capable, passionate, lifelong readers.
9. Reading skills and motivation factors are synergistic.

I will expand on these considerations. For each one, take the time to think about your own classroom, your students, your reading practices, and the books and resources you bring to the learning environment you create for students.

1. Sometimes Reading Is Hard

It is a misconception to think that learning to read is easy. Or that struggle in reading should be avoided. Neuroscientists tell us that reading is neither natural nor innate. Through something called neuroplasticity, we must force our brains to form circuits that allow us to read. The process is a long one, and the struggle should be viewed as natural and necessary. Everyone who is a reader has had to *learn* to read.

Notice the difference between these two statements: "Sometimes reading is hard" and "Maria is a struggling reader." When we say the first statement, we help teachers and students understand that challenges are a normal part of reading and that these challenges do not mean there is something wrong with the reader. When we acknowledge that sometimes reading is hard, the implication is that teachers and students can work together to figure out what to do next.

If struggle is necessary to learn to read, you can maintain the struggle without overwhelming students by applying John Hattie's Goldilocks principle (2012). We must make sure the reading we ask students to do is "not too hard and not too easy." This, Hattie says, will help to inspire confidence and provide a safety net. Most students must learn between 3000 and 4000 words every school year. It can be daunting for students to face so much new and difficult vocabulary, challenging concepts, and complex expository text structures all at once. It can result in a decrease in motivation for reading altogether. Finding a balance between reading success and reading challenge is key.

> Sometimes we don't tell students that they will face more complex reading as they move up the grades, or worse, we don't prepare them for the challenge.

Sometimes Teaching Reading Is Hard, Too

The simple view of reading (SVR) is making a comeback these days, and its very name implies that teaching reading is easy. On the one hand this view upholds the undisputed importance of helping students develop specific reading skills, particularly the systematic and explicit teaching of decoding for the purpose of comprehending text. Few teachers would disagree that these skills are crucial. On the other hand, SVR negates the experience many of us have had in teaching reading to hundreds of students over the years that not every student learns to read in the same way.

The pushback on SVR has been rising. The idea that learning to read is a simple combination of decoding ability and linguistic comprehension, defined as listening comprehension, has been around since the mid-1980s. Today, however, researchers and teachers tell us that SVR is an incomplete answer. They assert that additional factors must be considered. According to researcher Michelle Hagerman, for example, the SVR does not account for variables such as student motivation, interest, background knowledge, knowledge of comprehension strategies, text structure, and the reading context.

Teachers know that not all children and youth come into reading in exactly the same way or at the same time. So there cannot be just one universal, easy-to-roll-out recipe for teaching reading. I am persuaded by research that supports the observation that, "the differences among individuals and groups, their practices, their interactions, and the unpredictability that accompanies being human disrupts the possibility of narrow and universally applicable solutions for helping all students become readers" (Compton-Lilly, Mitra, Guay, & Spence, 2020).

I believe it makes sense to adopt a nuanced and expanded approach of SVR that acknowledges the complexity of reading, the diverse nature of the students we teach, and the complex nature of comprehension in learning to read. It may make teaching reading more of a challenge, but, in my view, it also brings more success.

2. Structures of Language Support Reading Instruction

You do not need to be a language expert to appreciate that reading is all about getting a handle on the structures of language. Knowing even a little bit about the structures of language will help you to understand teaching reading more deeply. Looking back on it now, I realize that I was lucky to begin teaching Grade 1 with a background in modern languages. I still felt lost in those first few months when I was teaching reading, but it started to dawn on me that how I learned my second language was remarkably similar to how those six-year-olds in my class were learning their first language. My students were learning the structures of language without necessarily being aware of it, and without me knowing it for a while, too.

What I have discovered is that when teachers know the structures of language, they are able to see the "why" behind certain instructional practices and strategies. Let's have a look at these structures to see exactly what our students are learning about language when they learn to read.

- **phonology**: study of the patterns of sounds in a language
- **semantics**: study of word meanings
- **syntax**: study of how words are ordered to convey meaning
- **morphology**: study of the structure of words
- **pragmatics**: study of how language is used in specific situations

We know that language has a **phonological structure**, which simply means that languages are based on recognizing patterns of sounds. These distinct units of sound are called "phonemes." So, to learn language, children must become aware of the sounds around them (in oral language and in print). They must become familiar with these sounds, use them, and learn what those sounds symbolize and mean. A young child singing a nursery rhyme like "Baa, Baa, Black Sheep" is learning to hear and make the /b/ sound and to associate that sound with the words *baa* and *black*. This type of oral work with language is important before and during the introduction of written work. A child who has experience hearing and making the sound /b/ will more easily be able to associate that sound when he or she is introduced to the symbol for that sound in print: the letter *b*.

As teachers, we are also aware that all language has a **semantic structure**. This refers to the meaning that language holds for speakers and listeners. Children, before coming to school, learn language and meaning. For instance, a toddler makes an utterance that the parent or caregiver assumes means "cracker" and offers the child a cracker. The child shakes his head no, and repeats his utterance, and again a cracker is offered and declined. Finally, the child makes a third attempt, and this time points to the cookie jar and is rewarded with a cookie. It has taken a bit of time, but the child has learned to use body language to make his meaning known. Given more time—and a parent who uses the word *cookie* repetitively but meaningfully—the child will learn to say the word *cookie* to achieve the same purpose.

Children come to school using language to make their needs known in a world mostly comprised of talking. At school, they learn to make sense of written language. But just pointing at a word, like pointing at the cookie jar, will not bring success with learning written language. The teacher, like the parent, must work with the child to make meaning of early reading experiences. The teacher says,

"Look at the first letter. Let's make the sound that goes with that letter." The child makes the /b/ sound. "Let's blend it with the next sound." The child, together with the teacher, blends /b/.../i/.../g/, slowly increasing the speed until the child recognizes and says, "big." The teacher follows up by saying "Show me something that is big." And the child might point at a picture of an elephant or stretch their arms out wide to show they know what *big* means. Just as in oral language, it has taken a bit of time. But the child has learned to make meaning from print.

All language has a **syntactical structure**. This refers to how words and phrases are put together to create meaning. For those of us who learn a second language, we figure out quickly that sentences in the second language are rarely put together, or structured, in the same way as our first language. For instance, I might say this sentence in English, "I live in the green house." But, when I speak French, I say, "J'habite à la maison verte." The word *green* comes before the word *house* in English, but *verte* comes after *maison* in French. That is what is referred to as the syntax, or grammar, of language.

A component of syntax is **morphology**, which is the study of word parts. Morphology refers to the internal structure of words, often referred to as morphemes or word parts. It should be noted that morphemes are the smallest unit of meaning in language. The word *cat* is a morpheme but so are *re-*, *-ed*, and *geo-*. The suffix *-ed*, for example, conveys past tense. Students are encouraged to figure out new and unfamiliar words by looking for word parts such as roots, prefixes, and suffixes to help with meaning and pronunciation.

Why does syntax matter in teaching reading? Intuitively, you know the rules of language, but your students are still learning these rules. They need to learn how sentences are written, how words are ordered to make sense, how word parts change meaning, and how punctuation is used to convey different meanings. By teaching students these conventions, you help students comprehend what they read, whether it is a science textbook, a short story, a recipe, a poster, or a play.

I will add that having knowledge about the differences of syntax from one language to another is immensely helpful when working with students who are English language learners (ELL). When you know what language a student speaks or hears at home, you can better identify what aspects of English syntax might be unfamiliar.

Lastly, language has a **pragmatic structure**. The language we use shifts according to circumstances. For instance, you may speak to your teaching colleagues more formally in the context of a staff meeting than you might when you go out for dinner together. Speakers adjust their language to suit their surroundings. Just as listeners understand a speaker best if they consider the context (staff meeting or dinner party), so do readers understand text best if they take into account the genre or purpose of the text.

It is valuable for you to know the language structures so that you can support your students' reading development with a greater understanding of the task they face each and every day in your classroom.

3. The Components of Reading Need to Be Taught Daily

When I ask successful reading teachers what they emphasize in teaching reading, virtually all say that they plan their program and lessons around decoding, fluency, vocabulary, and comprehension. These four critical areas are referred

Your students need to learn how sentences are written, how words are ordered to make sense, how word parts change meaning, and how punctuation is used to convey different meanings. By teaching students these conventions, you help them comprehend what they read.

to as the "components of reading" by the National Reading Panel report (2000). The report identifies these as the four essential components of effective reading instruction, adding that there are many different approaches to teaching them.

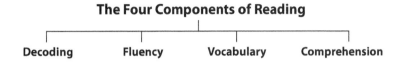

The Four Components of Reading

Decoding   Fluency   Vocabulary   Comprehension

The four essential components of reading were first described by the National Reading Panel in the United States.

It is not uncommon to see posters and charts in classrooms listing the reading components that guide teachers' instruction. I have seen them sometimes in the image of a flower, with one of the reading components printed on each petal, sometimes as a pyramid, and sometimes as the pillars of reading instruction. They remind me of the poster we often saw in classrooms called "The Writing Process"—a visual reminder of what matters in teaching writing. Of course, posters without action are not helpful. The first step is knowing what the components of reading are, why they matter, and how they are essential to teaching reading.

Decoding. Decoding involves two major skills: phonemic awareness and phonics knowledge. Phonemic awareness is the ability to hear and play with sounds in language. Phonics knowledge is understanding of letter-sound correspondence—which letters or letter combinations correlate to which sounds. Decoding involves putting together phonemic awareness and phonics knowledge to read words. This component is the focus of Chapter 2.

Fluency. Fluency is the ability to read "like you speak." It refers to the accuracy, rate, and expression of reading. Fluent readers decode words automatically, a process sometimes referred to as sight reading. Fluency provides a bridge to comprehension: when students give the majority of their cognitive attention to decoding words (which takes a great deal of time and effort), they are less able to devote attention to understanding what they read (comprehension). Fluency is the focus of Chapter 3.

Vocabulary. Vocabulary refers to the collection of words that students can read and understand. As students build their vocabulary repertoire, they are more likely to read fluently and with understanding. This component is the focus of Chapter 4.

Comprehension. Comprehension is the ability to understand and interpret what is read. It may lead to action on the part of the reader. This component is the focus of Chapter 5.

Although the reading components are separated one from the other for the purpose of discussion in this book, they are nonetheless inextricably woven together. Although they stand alone, each one supports the others. For instance, when a Grade 2 student expands her vocabulary, she can read more fluently, which lets her focus her attention more readily on what the text means.

4. Every Teacher Is a Reading Teacher

Once they are school-aged, students are asked to read every day, both inside and outside of school. On the very first day of school, students are often prompted to find their names on coat racks, on desks and tables, and on attendance-taking charts. From there, the need to be able to read increases exponentially.

We need to recognize that for some of our students, the demand to read brings emotions like stress, fear, and worry that escalate throughout the year because the demands of reading only increase. Without support, these students may not develop good reading skills. These students may make their way through the grades and continue to find reading hard. There is hope, however, if every teacher they encounter is a reading teacher, regardless of the grade or the discipline they teach.

Even when we are unaware that we teach reading, we still do. Print is so pervasive that teachers cannot help but pass along messages about reading to their students. No teacher is exempt.

- The band teacher displaying posters of labelled musical instruments throughout the music room is teaching new vocabulary.
- The physical education teacher who creates instructional posters at individual stations, with terms like *strength, circuit, abdominal, aerobic,* and *agility,* is using reading to support instruction.
- In science, mathematics, and social studies, teachers help students navigate textbooks, maps, instructions, digital tools, and other resources, all of which require the skill of reading.

Reading in any discipline adds to students' knowledge. If we remember that, as teachers, we are all in the knowledge-building endeavor together, we can support each other and our students to develop both the skills and the factors of motivation to become better readers. Two teachers describe the situation in many higher-level mathematics, social studies, and science classrooms.

> We all know that reading is important and transfers to all subject areas and it is an important life skill. Most teachers aren't "trained"—at least they don't think they are—so they don't know where to start. So they don't.
> —*Grade 6 teacher Jason*

And,

> Many teachers at my school are concerned that students' lower reading abilities are getting in the way of accessing content in courses like social studies and science. Students who don't know how to read textbooks or whose reading levels are too low to be able to comprehend the text are problematic in content-driven courses.
> —*Grade 8 teacher Holly*

The good news is that reading development never really ends. In grade school, high school, college, or university, we all continue to develop our reading skills, expand our reading interests, and find new reasons to read well into adulthood. I asked my senior-level pre-service teachers the question, "Are you a better reader now than you were in your first year of university?" They invariably and emphatically say, "yes." I follow up, "How do you know?" They say, "In my first year, I didn't maintain a reading schedule and I fell behind. Now I schedule time to read every day." Or "I learned to reread sections and use note-taking and write out questions to help me understand my reading." And "I keep a file on my computer with the new vocabulary I learn in each course. Then I can review it before

Victor Hugo once wrote, "To learn to read is to light a fire; every syllable that is spelled out is a spark." That's the job of all teachers.

exams." These students are motivated to do well in their courses, and they use the components of reading without even realizing it. Their responses show that reading continues to develop through effort and intention.

Teachers at all levels can turn the tide by making sure that their classroom environment, their resources, and their instruction motivate students. If you have not thought of yourself as a teacher of reading up until now, it is not too late. I am not suggesting that biology teachers need to throw away the microscopes and leap onto a desk, as Robin Williams did in *Dead Poets Society*, and shout "Carpe Diem!" But the teacher in this film did say, "No matter what anybody tells you, words and ideas can change the world." Teachers of all disciplines and grade levels can get behind that. Better readers lead to better learners.

5. Meaningful Relationships Are Key

No meaningful learning occurs without meaningful relationships. My trusted subject-matter experts all agreed that, as reading teachers, we all need to have meaningful relationships with our students if we expect they will learn from us and from each other. Cast your mind back to recall your favorite teachers. You may remember someone who helped you learn to play an instrument, or someone who suggested a book that you might like, or even a teacher who said you were a talented writer. Jaana Juvonen's (2007) work on social motivation tells us,

> Of school-based social relationships, teacher support is probably the most salient. When students feel supported and respected by their teachers, they are presumed to comply with the expectations and norms set by instructors and engage in the behaviors endorsed by these authority figures. When students lack a bond or do not get along with a teacher, students are presumed to disengage themselves from school-related activities and the institution. (p. 200)

Teachers know that if they want to teach reading, they have to get to know their students. And they have to help their students get to know them. Doing so pays massive dividends in reading improvement. Positive relationships build trust, psychological safety, and motivation. They even improve student behavior. As a teacher, I am able to motivate students as readers when I know what and how they are thinking. For instance, when I find out that ten-year-old Lucas filled out a reading-interest inventory saying that he loves hockey, I can follow up with him by saying, "I know you like hockey, Lucas, and I thought you might like to read this book called, *Rocket Blues* by David Skuy. Maybe you could read the first five pages and let me know what you think about it." This approach lets Lucas know that I learned something important about him and adjusted my instruction to make reading more interesting to him.

A word about working with older students is warranted here. Adolescent readers may be afraid that their teachers or their peers will judge their reading weaknesses harshly. Many students cannot help but compare themselves with their peers, so they recognize the differences in reading capability. Those dealing with reading difficulties will simply avoid reading. Building trust with adolescent students is essential. Students need to know that they will not be singled out in class or embarrassed as readers. Popcorn reading—or however it is referred to in classrooms—should be tossed out. In this practice, students take turns reading aloud. The *only* time it could be used is when students have a chance to practice what

Teachers know that if they want to teach reading, they have to get to know their students. And they have to help their students get to know them.

they will read aloud beforehand. Reading aloud is explored further in upcoming chapters.

One-on-one conversations to develop positive relationships are the answer when working with teens; these sessions help teachers and students get to know one another in a genuine way. I have enough experience working with adolescents to know that most are reticent to share anything about themselves if they detect superficiality. But brief conversations in the hallway before and after class can be used to build trust and gather information. You can then help steer them to reading material that might better match their interests. Finally, by understanding where students are at, you can help them to focus on their own improvement. For example, you might recommend small-group instruction with opportunities to talk and discuss texts to better meet some students' reading needs. You could only know to make this kind of instructional decision if you know your students as readers. Getting to know your readers, therefore, is a priority.

6. Students Need Good Reasons to Read

Now let's consider, as my subject-matter experts did, what happens when the components of reading are woven together with the factors of motivation needed for reading: confidence, interest and enjoyment, choice, dedication, and collaboration.

When I say that every teacher, at some point, wonders "How do I teach reading?" hovering in the background is another question: "How do I cultivate a love of reading?" This question is just as important as the first because you cannot create readers by simply giving them the skills to read. Students need to want to read. They need to see reading as purposeful, valuable, and enjoyable.

When you talk to the book lovers in your classroom, what do they say they love about reading? Ajla Grozdanic from the Save the Children organization asked elementary-aged children from around the world why they love to read. Here are some of their responses, which identify them all as motivated readers:

- "I love to read because the pictures and stories help me to imagine that I am somewhere else."—Nevaeh, 7
- "I like to read because there are new adventures all the time."—Brandon, 11
- "Because my mama likes to read."—Kayla, 8
- "I love to read because it helps me learn."—Hayden, 8
- "It is fun, and I learn my ABCs from books."—Emilee, 3 (Save the Children, 2013)

When students say that reading is boring, difficult, or overwhelming—or they just can't find a good book—they just won't read. So motivating students to want to read is as important as helping them develop the skills to read. When students want to read, their levels of engagement improve. Motivated readers remember how a book moved them, made them feel, or connected them with others in some way. They will put in the effort, persist, and be enthusiastic about reading, even when the reading gets hard, as it will do at some point in every student's life.

Teachers attentive to factors of motivation watch their students closely and monitor their feelings toward reading. They ask questions such as the following while watching their students.

- Do my students choose to read when they are given free time?
- Do they talk to me about what they are reading?
- Do they avoid reading?

Every teacher, at some point, wonders, "How do I teach reading?" Hovering in the background is another question: "How do I cultivate a love of reading?"

- Do they show negative behavioral or emotional reactions to reading?

Teachers' answers to these questions help them determine how they work with their students' unique reading strengths and challenges.

Students Who Do Not Like to Read	Students Who Do Like to Read
When you see one or more of the following, you have a student who *does not* like to read.	When you see one or more of the following, you have a student who *does* like to read.
• The student does not have strong reading skills and does not use strategies to self-monitor her understanding or self-correct when text doesn't make sense. • The student appears uninterested in what he reads. • The student finds the reading material too hard or overwhelming. • The student views reading as a task to do when assigned. • The student does not see a reason for reading. • The student has many activities that compete for her attention, and reading does not measure up.	• The student is good at reading and can self-monitor their understanding by pausing while reading to use letter-sound relationships, to use context clues, and to chunk root words. • The student has confidence and self-belief in their abilities. • The student connects with what they are reading. • The student likes to learn about topics by reading about them. • The student notices when others they admire read a book. • The student likes to talk with others about their reading.

In Kim's Classroom: Finding Just the Right Book

Teacher Kim shared with me her experience of observing Shay, an affable and active ten-year-old in her Grade 6 class. Shay loved to tinker and make things with found objects: pencils, erasers, elastics, anything he could get his hands on. Shay also seemed uninterested in reading until one day when Kim read aloud to the class from Philip Roy's *Submarine Outlaw*. The main character is Alfred, who, with the help of the owner of a junkyard, builds his own one-person submarine. Alfred's antics while building the submarine and being on the ocean are suspenseful, hilarious, and unexpected.

It is not surprising that Shay could identify with Alfred and his need to make something new and unique. Luckily for Shay, *Submarine Outlaw* was the first book in a series of eight by Roy. After being inspired by his teacher's read aloud, Shay was motivated to read more. He began reading the rest of the series on his own.

7. Teachers Must Be Readers

I remember the day in my Language and Learning in Teacher Education course when I made a statement to a group of pre-service teachers: "All teachers need to be readers." There was a moment of shocked silence and then, slowly but surely, the students began sharing stories of losing interest in reading, of replacing reading with other activities, of struggling as readers and avoiding it whenever possible, and of finding reading increasingly less interesting and more difficult for them as they moved through the grades. In other words, they did not find reading either worthwhile or inviting—and certainly not something to do for fun.

I had to change this. By addressing the benefits of reading for them and for their students, I began to shift their perceptions about the value of reading. They came to understand that teachers who read for pleasure are great reading role models for their students. If they read, then they can credibly speak about how they read, what and when they read, and, most importantly, how they handle reading challenges. They are able to share strategies they use to help them as readers and to talk about what they are learning from reading.

I assert that teachers in all disciplines should be readers by example. They can help students find books they want to read and help them pair up with reading friends (others who have similar reading interests). I am thinking of Grade 4 art teacher, Krista, who loved the book *Smile* by Raina Telgemeier. Krista loved the book so much she shared it with her students, and several of them became friends specifically because they shared an interest in the artwork of the book. For teachers, reading is a way to learn, to find connections between their reading and their teaching, a way to relax and to address their own wellness, and, perhaps most important, to show students how reading can matter, personally.

Teachers in all disciplines should be readers by example.

What Have You Read Lately?

A few years ago, I started all my new courses for pre-service teachers and professional learning workshops with the question, "What have you read lately?" I always follow up by saying, "Anything goes. It's just a way for us to see that we all read every day and that we have reading interests just like our students do." I am clear that no one will judge anyone's choices. Whenever I did this, I found that the energy in the room increased. Whether I was working with pre-service teachers or teachers, they became animated and talked excitedly about the reading they had been doing. These conversations continued throughout our time together.

Talking about reading served three purposes.

- It energized the group.
- It allowed connections to be made between and among us.
- It reminded us that reading generates good feelings.

Imagine if administrators began staff meetings, teachers started the school week, and students began group work with the question, "What have you read lately?" What would be your reply?

We are all readers. And teachers are more aware than most of their own reading strengths and challenges. Why not use those real experiences to be role models for students? Students need to know that there are all kinds of readers and that this is as true for adults as it is for them. You can tell your students what kind of reader you are and what kind of reader you have been in the past, so they can see that it is not a stagnant condition. It is good for students to know you have overcome—or still struggle with—reading challenges.

Let's look at an example. I remember being an avid reader right up to Grade 6, and then one day in school my teacher quizzed me in front of the whole class about a part of the story I had just read. I froze and couldn't remember details from the story—I hummed a bit and tried to make a joke, but ultimately, I think, my love for reading died right then and there. I read for school and university in the ensuing years, but I did not see myself as a real reader until much later. It was only after I became a teacher, when I would watch and help my young Grade 1 students learn to read, that I became a passionate reader again myself.

I recall when a new teacher confided in me that it had been years since she had read a book for pleasure. She was just beginning her career as a Grade 4 teacher. She told me, "I do read what I need and want to read. I read recipes, magazines, and favorite social media sites, but a book? Never." I told her not to see her lack of reading a novel in the past as a barrier to teaching reading but as a starting point. The first step for this teacher was to identify her interests and then to find books that she could read on her own (and later with her students) to help her engage in deep and meaningful reading again.

Another enthusiastic and caring high school teacher, Jose, told me he was a reluctant reader growing up. But he had been a talented soccer player. Jose confided in me that if a teacher, any teacher, had suggested he read a book featuring soccer or one of his soccer heroes, he probably would have wanted to read that book. Jose said that he only rediscovered reading once he started teaching and that he now reads constantly with his students and his own children.

It is quite possible that as a teacher you may have struggled as a reader in school, leaving you unenthusiastic and a bit fearful about teaching reading. Jennifer was one such teacher and she says that it took years for her to develop a positive reader identity. She viewed teaching, however, as a way to find, use, and teach reading strategies to strengthen the reading skills of both her *and* her students. Today Jennifer tells me that she sees her students experiencing some of the same challenges that she experienced as a child. Jennifer is honest and straightforward in telling her students about her reading challenges, an attitude that helps her students meet their own challenges with a healthy attitude. Teachers at all levels can turn the tide by making sure that their classroom environment, their resources, and their instruction motivates students.

8. Reading Engagement Leads to the Goal: Capable, Passionate, Lifelong Readers

Reading engagement means full participation in the act of reading; it involves knowing what you are doing, why you are doing it, wanting to do it, and giving it your all.

What does reading engagement look like? You probably see it happen in your classroom every day. When students are genuinely interested in what they are doing, they put in the effort to do the work, they respond enthusiastically to the task, they eagerly interact with one another, and they persist in the task without being reminded to do so.

Engagement is also described as flow, meaning it is a kind of non-stop activity characterized by absorption, enthusiasm, and, importantly, success. We all know what it feels like to be completely focused and immersed in an activity. That's flow.

Teaching Tip

Take your own reading pulse. Ask,
- How often do I read aloud to my students?
- How often do I read on my own for pleasure?
- How often do I read professional learning resources?
- How often do I talk to colleagues about professional learning resources?

Students engaged in reading are
- involved
- connected
- hooked
- interested
- deep in thought
- captivated
- engrossed
- focused
- intent

Although I now primarily teach pre-service teachers at a university, I truly enjoy the opportunity to be a guest reader in grade-school classrooms for special events like World Read Aloud Day in February, International Literacy Day in September, and One Book, One School initiatives.

After reading a story or an excerpt from a story, my favorite question to ask students is, "What did you think of that?" The question is deliberately open-ended, seeking students' immediate responses about anything related to the reading. It's a perfect question to elicit students' engagement with the story.

On one such occasion, I read the picture book *Perfect Man* by Troy Wilson and Dean Griffiths. It is the story of a super-hero named Perfect Man who gives up his title and status to seek "another way to save the world." Readers of this wonderful book begin making inferences and predictions early in the story that Perfect Man will become the main character's third-grade teacher. The book does not divulge any certainty around this question, and students' comments and questions clearly show the connections they are making with the story.

One student said, "That IS Perfect Man! He stops the bullies in the playground." Another added, "No, he is just a good teacher." (That's me smiling at that comment.) One student asked, "How did he know that Michael wanted to be a writer?" Another student responded, "Look at the page where the teacher says he is his biggest fan."

The conversation continued for several minutes until all students had shared their questions and comments. One student added, "I think he is going to go back to being Perfect Man … 'cause he could fly then!" Students were fully engaged in this conversation about the book. With just one genuine question, I had prompted students to share with me and one another their feelings about the characters, what happened in the story, and the wonderings they had. They even offered alternative endings when they were not pleased with what occurred in the book. To me, that is what reading engagement looks like.

Reading engagement might look different in a mathematics class than it does in a home economics class, but the best way to find out if your students are engaged in reading is to ask yourself the following questions. Share the questions with a colleague and talk together about how to support reading engagement with your students. Sharing ideas can help you make reading engagement the goal of your reading instruction.

What Does Reading Engagement Look Like in Your Classroom?

Think of a time when your students appeared fully engaged in reading something in your classroom.

- What was happening?
- Why do you think this activity was engaging for your students?
- How were students showing their use of the skills of reading?
- How were students showing motivational aspects of reading?

Think of a time when your students appeared less engaged in reading than you would have hoped.

- What was happening?
- Why do you think this activity was less engaging for your students?

Engagement: The Key to Achieving Your Goal

It is only by sparking reading engagement that we have a chance to light the fire that is a lifelong passion for reading.

Why do so many teachers strive for reading engagement? Why do they take such satisfaction in witnessing engaged reading? Perhaps because they like to see evidence that their instructional practices to develop students' reading skills and levels of motivation are working.

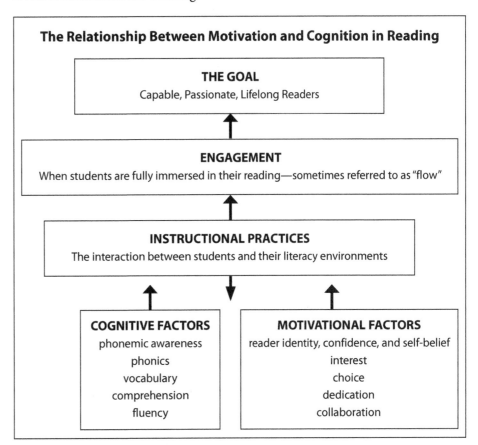

The pathway from instruction to engagement creates lifelong readers.

9. Reading Skills and Motivation Factors Are Synergistic

Motivation to read and reading skills make a magical combination. Nancy Frey, John Guthrie, and other researchers tell us that we have known for a long time about the interconnected relationship between reading skills and motivation factors for reading. Unfortunately, knowledge about teaching reading skills and motivating reading have been kept distinct, each in its own silo.

Frey says that, if we are to successfully engage students in reading, we must address these together, from day one. No more silos. While teachers are familiar with what is meant by the term *motivation*, they know less about how exactly to support it in the classroom. What are the motivation factors that make a real difference to readers?

John Guthrie tells us that engaged readers can overcome barriers related to achievement, parental education, and family income. Teachers invest their time and effort teaching reading skills, so students become capable readers. But if they neglect the development of motivation factors, their efforts may be for naught.

The factors of motivation I explore in this book for students as readers are

1. **Confidence**: "I know how to read."
2. **Interest**: "I like to read about _____."
3. **Choice**: "I like to choose my books."
4. **Dedication**: "Sometimes it's hard, but I just try to figure it out."
5. **Collaboration**: "I like to talk with my friends about books."

Because the factors of motivation interact synergistically with the skills of reading, it makes sense to provide reading instruction that supports both motivation and reading skills at the same time. Otherwise, we may fall short of meeting students' expectations. I believe this is what Janet Emig, Professor Emeritus at Rutgers University, meant when she said that it is "magical thinking" to believe that what is taught is what is learned. She is referring to the gap created when our instruction does not meet the learner's needs. When that happens, despite all our best intentions, students do not benefit from our reading instruction.

To learn and apply reading skills, your students need to have confidence in themselves as readers. They need to know that they can learn to read and that *you know* they can learn to read. Some students grow up believing they cannot learn to read. Without a belief in themselves, they may behave in ways—mostly out of fear, anger, and insecurity—that make it impossible to provide instruction that will help them.

You have likely observed students who will pretend to read. Perhaps they work with others who carry them through an assignment, or they avoid reading in other ways. Perhaps they act out in class. Any one of these behaviors, let alone a combination of them, make it hard to teach these students reading. But in my experience, all does not have to be lost. We only need to remember that reading skills and factors of motivation are two sides of the same coin. When students want to read and they enjoy it, their reading skills improve. As their reading skills improve, they want to read more.

As adults, we read what interests us. We make our own choices about what to read and we decide when to read and for how long. When I make these decisions, I devote my time and attention to reading the books I buy or borrow. But students don't always buy or borrow the books they read. More often they have little choice about what they read. Teachers will always be assigning readings in school, but if we want students to value reading, we have to provide opportunities for them to find books that interest them. If they choose the book, they are more likely to follow through and read it.

During my years as a professor of education, I have had the opportunity to prepare, interact with, and observe the work of hundreds of pre-service teachers working in classrooms during their practicums. One of my pre-service teachers, who was working in a middle school, recently tweeted this message to me, "I

> To learn and apply reading skills, your students need to know that they can learn to read and that *you know* they can learn to read.

read this book, *Punching the Air* by Ibi Zoboi and Yusef Salaam, when I was on a hunt for a book that I could recommend to one of my students. He was really uninterested in reading, but he loved music and was always dancing at his desk. I suggested he read this book like a rap, and the next time I saw him there was a bookmark in the middle of the book! He told me it 'changed reading for him.'"

So, how do you avoid the silos, and instead address reading skills and motivation factors concurrently? How do you support your students to be passionate, lifelong readers? First, as my trusted subject-matter experts advised, you must possess a clear and profound understanding of the components of reading. This knowledge will translate to practice every single day. It means that you will know

- that **what** you teach is important to reading
- **why** you select certain reading materials and resources
- **how** to choose skills and strategies to emphasize with your students

Second, you need to examine your teaching philosophy, classroom environment, and teaching strategies. You must constantly ask yourself, "Does my practice provide real reasons to read?"

You can marry these two approaches into one, to help your students develop a reading capability for both learning and pleasure.

Your Key Takeaways

Here are the key ideas we explored in this chapter on teaching reading.

- Reading must be learned.
- You can learn to teach reading.
- The components of reading are decoding (phonics and phonemic awareness), fluency, vocabulary, and comprehension.
- The motivation factors for reading are confidence, interest, choice, dedication, and collaboration.
- Teaching reading requires a synergy between the components of reading and the motivation factors.
- These nine major considerations provide a strong foundation for teaching reading:

    1. Sometimes reading is hard.
    2. Structures of language support reading instruction.
    3. The components of reading need to be taught daily.
    4. Every teacher is a reading teacher.
    5. Meaningful relationships are key.
    6. Students need good reasons to read.
    7. Teachers must be readers.
    8. Reading engagement leads to the goal: capable, passionate, lifelong readers.
    9. Reading skills and motivation factors are synergistic.

2

Decoding: On the Path to Fluency

In helping young children to become literate, it makes sense to encourage the development of phonemic awareness. However, we must avoid creating an environment in which children are drilled in phonemic awareness, especially if the associated activities are separate from regular classroom activities.

—Barbara Wasik, research scientist, 2001

Do you like to do jigsaw puzzles? Our family has always liked to complete puzzles, both jigsaw puzzles and crossword puzzles. As jigsaw puzzlers know, one of the first things to do when faced with a picture puzzle with hundreds if not thousands of pieces, is to turn all the pieces right side up and then make a separate pile of all the border pieces. This helps me to build a foundation for the puzzle, because I can assemble the edges and corners first and build from there.

Once the border takes shape, I fill the puzzle in. I like the feeling of confidence this puzzle strategy gives me. The border helps me keep the big picture in mind even in the early stages of building the puzzle. That is important, because the big picture gives me the motivation to keep working even when the puzzle is challenging. And, believe me, it can be challenging!

*Learning to read is like doing a puzzle. Building a foundation
(like the border of a puzzle) creates the motivation to keep going.*

You might see decoding referred to as *word identification* or *word study*. They all mean the same thing.

Learning to read is just like doing a puzzle. Early readers must build a foundation for reading on phonemic awareness and phonics knowledge. These two essential skills enable students of all ages to decode words. When students are young, they develop phonemic awareness when they recognize sounds and connect those sounds with letters. They develop phonics knowledge when they connect those sounds and letters to written letters. Decoding is the translation of letters and letter combinations into sounds and into words. As students get older, the decoding skills learned earlier come into play as they encounter new and unfamiliar vocabulary and the texts that they read become more complex.

The Goals: Phonemic Awareness, Phonics Knowledge, the Alphabetic Principle, and Decoding

Phonemic awareness: Students hear, recognize, and work with the sounds of language. Phonemic awareness is developed through oral language. Teachers provide opportunities for students to learn

- syllable awareness
- rhymes
- alliteration

Phonics knowledge: Students learn that the letters or symbols of language correspond to sounds. Phonics knowledge is developed through written language. Teachers provide opportunities for students to learn

- initial and final consonants
- onsets and rimes
- blending
- segmenting
- replacing and manipulating sounds

The alphabetic principle: When phonemic awareness and phonics knowledge come together to help students learn to read and spell.

Decoding: Students use phonemic awareness, phonics knowledge, and other clues such as the grammar and syntax of a sentence, contextual clues, word parts, and familiarity with similar words to sound out, recognize, and correctly pronounce words. Teachers provide opportunities for students to learn

- root words
- prefixes and suffixes
- multisyllabic words
- common word syllable patterns (such as *-tion, -ing*, and *-ment*)

Before Children Read, They Talk

Our brains are hard-wired to learn to talk but not to read.

Our brains are hard-wired to learn to talk. This is not the case for reading. Humans have been talking much longer than we have been reading. Learning to read, however, depends on our innate ability to learn to talk. One of my favorite sayings from James Britton is, "Reading and writing float on a sea of talk." This tells us just how important talk is in the task of learning how to read and write.

A quiet classroom is not necessarily a good place for language to grow. Here are some of the ways that children learn to talk both at school and at home. They

- have meaningful conversations
- listen to others talk
- initiate talk well before they can form words
- ask questions
- repeat sounds over and over again
- play and make believe
- watch videos
- listen to and tell stories
- sing songs
- talk on the phone
- play rhyming games like "I spy" and "Inky-pinky"
- recite and act out nursery rhymes

Learning the Sounds of Language

Early talking experiences support students to use and make the sounds of language, any language, and eventually associate these with print. Through talk, children learn to hear and say sounds, or phonemes, that they will eventually learn to recognize in print.

Learning to talk is a glorious accomplishment. We would never say to a talking child, "You are learning your phonemes. Good for you!" Yet that is exactly what they are doing. And it is a crucial step in learning to read. Children need these talking experiences to build their phonemic awareness: their ability to hear, make, and manipulate the sounds of the language.

In Steven's Classroom: Fun Building Phonemic Awareness

I watched a lovely lesson to develop phonemic awareness unfold in a Kindergarten classroom. The teacher, Steven, and his students were singing the popular song, *Down by the Bay*. The song goes,

> Down by the bay
> Where the watermelons grow
> Back to my home
> I dare not go
> For if I do
> My mother will say
> "Did you ever you ever see a cat
> wearing a hat?"

Teacher Steven and his students continued singing verses with ever more rhyming words: *whale* and *tail*, *fly* and *tie*, *bear* and *hair*. Steven would pause just before the second rhyming word was sung. Students listened for the word they needed to rhyme and the pause, and then enthusiastically sang the new rhyming word. Then Steven would make up new lines and wait while his students came up with a new rhyming word. The rhymes became silly and fun.

Phonemic awareness is developed through oral activities like this one. These activities are meant to be fun, and students participate eagerly. But these activities have a serious purpose. They develop the listening-for-language skills needed to make sense of written language.

> **Teaching Phonemic Awareness, Phonics Knowledge, and Decoding**
>
> Phonemic awareness …
> - … is developed through oral activities.
> - … should be fun and game-like. Keep a sense of playfulness with language and avoid worksheets and drills.
> - … is achieved through stories, poems, and songs that have rhythm and rhyme.
> - … is developed through chanting, singing, and clapping activities.
> - … is supported by sharing high-quality, engaging literature.
> - … leads to fluency.
>
> Phonics knowledge …
> - … is taught through explicit, systematic instruction.
> - … begins with the sounds associated with letters and then moves to consonant-vowel-consonant patterns.
> - … is developed by segmenting words into sounds and blending those sounds.
> - … should be fun and game-like.
> - … is supported by sharing high-quality, engaging literature.
> - … leads to fluency.
>
> Decoding …
> - … is taught through explicit instruction.
> - … is supported by looking at patterns in written text, for instance, *-tion* in words like *transportation* and *locomotion*.
> - … is taught by learning about prefixes, suffixes, and multisyllabic words.
> - … should include the pronunciation of words.
> - … includes seeing similarities and differences in words with similar etymology, such as *define, definition*, and *definite*.
> - … is built by teaching segmentation of words (breaking words down into individual sounds or syllables).
> - … is understood in the context of reading.
> - … leads to fluency.

Code Breaking

Picture Alan Turing deciphering encrypted enemy communications during WWII. That's more or less what our children do as beginner readers.

Learning phonics is sometimes referred to as code breaking. Picture Alan Turing deciphering encrypted enemy communications during WWII. This act of translation is more or less what students do as beginning readers. They must learn to associate the 44 unique phonemes in the English language with combinations of the 26 letters of the English alphabet. The application of this knowledge in learning to read and spell is called the "alphabetic principle."

Until you watch children make these associations and see the proverbial light bulb turn on, it is hard to appreciate the incredible brain work involved in learning to read. Phonics knowledge depends on phonemic awareness, that is, students being able to hear and differentiate the different sounds in language.

You may find it useful to follow a systematic phonics program or create your own that includes a progression for teaching the letters and their associated sounds. I have always liked the timeless resource, *Spelling Through Phonics* by Marlene McCracken and Robert McCracken because it contains detailed instructions on how to teach decoding and spelling in a fun way that builds confidence. Students love practicing on individual whiteboards with sock erasers!

Today, you have many programs to choose from, including many that offer computer applications and games for group and independent practice. Phonics instruction, when accompanied by exposure to literature, or what I call "real reading," helps students to see the relationship between phonics and reading. It is important that a structured approach to decoding instruction integrates the language arts—reading, writing, listening, and speaking. In this way, instruction can and should be fun, engaging, and interactive. It may include singing, games such as bingo, matching activities, play with magnetic letters, use of colorful writing utensils, and computer games. I've even seen sand and shaving cream used effectively for writing practice!

A Structured Approach to Decoding

A structured approach to teaching decoding is required in the primary grades. Most such programs include the following.

1. **Explicit instruction linked to reading**. You clearly and deliberately explain key skills.
2. **Phonology**. You plan lessons that focus on the sounds and letters of language, using such techniques as rhyming, clapping syllables, and counting words in a spoken sentence.
3. **Sound-symbol relationships**. You use a planned sequence of instruction that is both sequential and cumulative. You begin by teaching foundational skills such as recognizing consonant sounds and vowel sounds, and then progressing to more advanced skills such as blending sounds and segmenting words.
4. **Morphology**. You provide syllable instruction and help students see word parts as they learn to read.
5. **Syntax**. You provide opportunities for students to learn about word order and sentence structure.
6. **Semantics**. You embed phonics instruction into a rich language context by highlighting the relationship among words to create meaning.
7. **Opportunities for writing**. Through daily writing, students practice and show their developing knowledge of sound-symbol relationships and spelling.
8. **Monitoring students' progress**. Regular diagnostic assessment is crucial because, once students have developed decoding skills, it is important to move them along as readers.
9. **Interventions, as necessary**. Interventions are provided to students in small groups or one to one to meet their specific learning needs. Students requiring this extra support might include English language learners (ELL), students with language disabilities, and students with a diagnosis of dyslexia.

Let's look at an example progression that you might follow to develop students' phonics knowledge.

Decoding can be fun. I've even seen sand and shaving cream used effectively for writing practice!

Teaching Tip
Regular diagnostic assessment is crucial because, once students have developed decoding skills, it is important to move them along as readers.

- You start by telling students that they are going to use what they know about letters and sounds to learn to read some new words.
- You introduce the initial and final consonant sounds in short words, and then progress to an exploration of consonant-vowel-consonant (CVC) words such as /m/ /a/ /t/ and /t/ /o/ /p/.
- You then help your students segment the words by s-t-r-e-t-c-h-i-n-g out their sounds in speech and then blending the sounds back together to read the words. The visual image of an elastic band goes a long way in helping students learn to stretch words as they say them.
- Once your students can sound out these CVC words on their own, you move on to words with more letters such as *stop* and *hand*.
- Finally, your students use their knowledge of letters and sounds to tackle more difficult words such as *light*, *shake*, and *back*. This group of words consist of onsets and rimes (An onset is the consonant sound that precedes the vowel. A rime is the vowel and any consonant sounds that follow)—as in *l-* and *-ight*, *sh-* and *-ake*, and *b-* and *-ack*—and are often referred to as word families by both teachers and students.

After students become familiar with common onsets and rimes and know how to manipulate the sounds at the beginning of these, they will be able to decode many new words.

When Guessing Doesn't Cut It

It is important to watch students as they are involved in these kinds of code-breaking activities. I recall observing a young child in a Montessori Kindergarten classroom use three large cardboard letters she had created herself to make words.

- She had cut out one card in the shape of the letter *m* and had glued pieces of macaroni to it.
- A second card was cut out as a letter *a* and had a picture of an apple on it.
- The third card was cut into a letter *t*. The child had drawn a picture of a truck on it.

The student's teacher asked her to make each letter sound, /m/ /a/ /t/, and then blend each sound together to make a new word. The child successfully read the word *mat*. Then off she went to another part of the classroom.

Curious to see what the girl would remember of the lesson, I called the student back a few minutes later. The letters were still arranged on the table. I asked her if she remembered the word she had made. She didn't hesitate but proudly announced that the word was *rug*.

In other words, the child took a guess. She did not even try to sound out the word.

You might be thinking, "So what? The meaning is still the same." But as students are faced with more text and more complicated text, it simply won't be efficient to just guess what words say. Although the child did guess the correct meaning, knowing the meaning had not been the point of the lesson. The point of the lesson was to decode the word, a skill that guessing does not require.

The letters and sounds provide clues in reading. We want students to learn to use those clues and apply their knowledge of letters and sounds to decode words.

This gives them a starting point when faced with new and unfamiliar words. This is how phonemic awareness and phonics knowledge lay the foundation for reading. The lesson? Don't allow for guessing. Make sure students are decoding every time.

Make It Fun

How can you make students aware of and excited about the big picture of learning to read? After all, you may know that decoding is a foundational skill needed to read successfully, but your students might not know that. When they are buried in the difficult brainwork of building their phonics knowledge, it might not feel very connected to the reading of meaningful text. There is a reason for the phrase "drill and kill"! Pernille Ripp reminds us,

> We're constantly reading for skill. We're constantly asking kids to do something with their reading, and then we wonder why they leave us and never pick up another book. They can't wait to get out of school so that they don't have to read. (2017)

At the beginning of this chapter, I suggested that building the foundation for reading was like putting together the border of a puzzle. As a person who enjoys doing jigsaw puzzles, I know that connecting the pieces will eventually lead to a complete big picture. That knowledge helps me to maintain my motivation when the puzzle gets hard. So remind your students continually about the goal of all their efforts.

In addition, you can make the journey fun. When I do puzzles, I really enjoy the challenge and satisfaction—and fun—of putting a thousand little squiggly pieces of cardboard together in just the right way. You may recall that in Steven's classroom phonemic awareness was developed through song and fun. Phonics knowledge can be approached in the same manner. Einstein once said, "Play is the highest form of research." There is no reason why students cannot research how language works through play. This is as true for older readers as it is for younger ones.

In a structured approach, decoding instruction should take the form of short, focused lessons that involve all your students and that don't take too long. To keep instruction fun and engaging, provide interactive game-like activities. Here are a few examples of techniques you can use.

- **Rhymes and songs**. Songs that provide rhymes, like "Bingo," "The Alphabet Song," "Five Green and Speckled Frogs," "I Know an Old Lady," and all the Raffi songs, are particularly good resources.
- **Games for students to play with partners and in small groups**. Fishing for letters, matching letters to sounds, matching words to pictures, online games, and name games are a few that you might use. (Name games will be explored in the next section of this chapter.)
- **Whiteboard spelling**. Students divide their individual whiteboards into four boxes and make two short lines along the bottom of each box a few centimetres apart. You ask students to write the letters associated with the sounds you make and then to hold up their whiteboards. Students advance to spelling short words and listening for and writing consonant blends.

Is Decoding for Older Readers Too?

The answer is absolutely! Students over the age of ten with limited phonics knowledge and English language learners are at a disadvantage when reading. These limitations will affect fluency, vocabulary knowledge, and comprehension. The texts middle and high school students need to read include specialized academic vocabulary and unfamiliar words. So phonics knowledge, or code-breaking, is important for older students too. Readers of all ages would find it helpful to sound out new words, look for familiar word parts, and break a word into its syllables—that is, if the lesson isn't boring!

We cannot treat older readers, however, in the same way that we do younger readers when it comes to phonics knowledge. Ivey and Baker warn us that if middle and high school teachers are going to adopt phonics programs, they might want to ask themselves these questions:

- How can I teach word knowledge to the students who really need it?
- How can I encourage the thoughtful reading of texts?
- Do my students get enough opportunities to read interesting materials that they can easily manage?
- Do my students find relevance in the reading they are asked to do in school? (Ivey & Baker, 2004)

For older readers, instruction should be both age appropriate and holistic. Assuming you are a high school teacher, let's look at how you might approach decoding of a word such as *geography*. This exercise would likely include a look at the structure of the word and a recognition of its Greek roots. You might help students break the word into two parts—*geo-* and *-graphy*—and apply what you know about these. *Geo-* is a prefix meaning "earth," and *-graphy* is a root word that means "field of study" or "related to writing." You might help students notice how *geography* is used in a sentence, as a way of helping them to make sense of its pronunciation and meaning.

In this example, we can see how phonemic awareness (the sounds of language) and phonics (knowledge of the letter/sound correspondences) go hand in hand to provide a foundation for students as they learn to read. These skills, together with knowledge about word origins, help older students read to learn.

Your decoding instruction, whether you teach younger or older students, should assist in the following:

- build students' self-confidence as readers
- assist them to see the purpose of their lessons
- help them find interest and enjoyment in reading
- support their dedication to the task of learning to read

Decoding instruction needs to be direct, explicit, and systematic. As Maryanne Wolf has said, decoding instruction "should never mean neglecting engagement with literature" (2018).

From Talk to Print

Some children appear to move seamlessly from the world of talk to the world of print. They possess a well-developed sense of phonemic awareness and basic phonics knowledge that together ease them into the task of decoding unfamiliar words. An interview with parents or guardians will likely reveal that they have shared books with family members, played rhyming games, or sung songs at home. These children typically have been exposed to language through hours and hours of bedtime stories and other literacy activities. They often write and draw on their own.

My daughter was an avid writer before she started Grade 1, creating stories, making signs, and writing notes. She had learned that words on a page were talk written down—she was learning to read by writing. It was therefore amusing (and a bit bothersome) that she announced after her first day in Grade 1, "Guess what, Mom. Mrs. MacDonald taught me to read today!"

Not all children, however, grow up in circumstances that prepare them so well for reading. And some children simply require the time and support a teacher can offer. You need to be prepared, therefore, to provide a strong foundation in phonemic awareness and phonics knowledge for those students who need it.

In Matthew's Classroom: But What Does It Say?

I observed one of my pre-service teachers, Matthew, as he read a book aloud to his Grade 2 students. The book was *That's (Not) Mine* by Anna Kang and illustrated by Christopher Weyant. What ensued illustrates what happens when children do not yet associate speech with print.

Matthew held up the book and asked his students to predict what the book might be about based on the title and cover. With this approach, he attended to an important component of reading: the well-known comprehension strategy of prediction. One student said, "It is going to be about a fight." Another added, "They both want to sit on the chair." Matthew told the students, "Those are great predictions. Let's see what happens."

Matthew then read the book to his students, pausing occasionally for them to comment, ask questions, or guess what would happen next.

When he finished reading the book, one little girl named Mandy said, "What did it say?" Matthew looked perplexed. He said, "But I read the book."

The student persisted, "But what did it say on the pages?" Matthew asked the student to come up and show him what she meant. Mandy got up and looked at the book. She opened the book and pointed to the words and said, "What does this say?"

That is the point when Matthew realized that Mandy had not understood that his speech *was* reading. He quickly recovered and said, "I am going to read the book again, and this time, I will point to the words while I read."

Matthew reread the book. Using a pointer this time, he showed when each of the characters was talking by pointing first at the character in the illustration and then pointing to the text on the page that corresponded to the dialogue spoken by that character.

Matthew's new approach satisfied Mandy and perhaps other students in the class who had not yet made a connection between speech and print. It demonstrates how younger students' perceptions of reading sometimes make learning to read hard. Mandy was clearly interested in the book, demonstrating motivation for reading, but she did not associate what was being said with reading, that is, until Matthew adjusted his approach to explicitly point to the characters and words in the book. Fortunately, Matthew noticed what was happening. He was able to show Mandy that speech and print are related.

> **Teaching Tip:** *Just Sing It!*
>
> Sing nursery rhymes and other songs that require students to listen to beginning sounds and change them (for example, "There was a farmer had a dog and Bingo was his name-o, B-I-N-G-O…"). You don't have to be a good singer to do this, just an enthusiastic one. The students will sing along. And someone in the class can usually carry a tune. Just follow that person! Here are a few other tips for helping with decoding.
>
> - Play rhyming games such as "Inky Pinky" and "Hickety Pickety."
> - Clap syllables while reading, chanting, or singing.
> - Count the sounds in words, like /c/ /a/ /t/ before you ask students to connect the sounds and letters.
> - Emphasize the relationship between learning decoding skills and learning to read the texts that students want to read.
> - Help students look for syllables that appear in multiple words, such as *-ing, -tion, -graphy, -ness, -ism,* and *-poly.*
> - Give students opportunities in small groups to say out loud the words they find difficult.

Love at First "Sight"

Many students come to school already knowing how to recognize some words by sight. These are words such as their own names, *Mom, Dad, stop* (if they have been encouraged to notice signs outside the window during car trips), a pet's name, *Nana, Poppa,* and other words that are important in their home environments. My personal favorite words students recognize are the words *love* and *like,* often appearing as *luv* and *lik* when students write them for themselves.

After students learn to recognize words quickly, or automatically, these words are called "sight words." In a sense, learning to read is a process of turning all words into sight words. Remember that every sight word was once an unfamiliar word. To make a word a sight word, you or your students must find a way to make it instantly recognizable. This is accomplished through activities and strategies such as making word walls together, word-picture matching games, reading signs together, using magnetic letters to make words and manipulate the sounds of those words, and giving read-alouds during which students can see and connect with the text.

Many sight words do not conform to alphabetic rules. Attempting to sound those words out, therefore, might not help a reader successfully identify the word. These are the kinds of words that we typically identify as early sight words—they must be put into memory without sounding out. Examples are words such as *they (thay), does (duz), like (lik), goes (goz), could (cud, cood), nice (nis), friend (frend), people (peepl), teacher (techer),* and many others that often take weeks if not months to learn to spell correctly and consistently.

Naturally knowing sight words helps the reader with fluency. If students must decode every word they are reading, the task becomes laborious, slow, and choppy and the reader may completely miss the meaning of the text. Being able to recognize words quickly, accurately, and effortlessly lets students speed up their reading and focus on comprehension. In the beginning, readers move at their own pace from a slow, sounding-out phase to a smooth, fluent phase. Be patient. Students need to know you believe in their ability to get there.

In a sense, learning to read is a process of turning all words into sight words.

Teaching Tip

Be up front with students about the strangeness of the English language. You might keep a list of sight words with the oddest spellings on a word wall and give it a heading:

- Doozys
- Snap Words
- Humdingers
- Dolch Sight Words
- Fry Words
- Wonder Words

In the past, I have asked my pre-service teachers if they think it is more important for students to recognize words on sight or to be able to sound out words. It is a bit of a trick question. <u>Students need to be able to do both: recognize sight words quickly and automatically *and* sound out unfamiliar words.</u>

If you think that the English language can be learned through decoding alone, I challenge you to read the following poem using just decoding. There are many exceptions to the alphabetic principle that students need to learn. I find it hard not to think of our students as little geniuses after reading this poem!

Brush Up Your English

By T. S. Watt

I take it you already know
Of tough and bough and cough and dough.
Others may stumble but not you,
On hiccough, thorough, lough, and through.
Well done! And now you wish, perhaps,
To learn of less familiar traps.

Beware of heard, a dreadful word
That looks like beard and sounds like bird,
And dead—it's said like bed, not bead.
For goodness's sake, don't call it deed!
Watch out for meat and great and threat:
They rhyme with suite and straight and debt.

A moth is not a moth in mother,
Nor both in bother, broth in brother,
And here is not a match for there,
Nor dear and fear for bear and pear,
And then there's dose and rose and lose—
Just look them up—and goose and choose,
And cork and work and card and ward,
And font and front and word and sword,
And do and go and thwart and cart.
Come, come, I've hardly made a start.

A dreadful language? Man alive,
I'd mastered it when I was five.

Marc is a ten-year-old boy in Grade 4 who tells his teacher, Kendra, that he likes mathematics "and a lot of other stuff, like sports" and that his favorite books are by Eric Walters because "he has good characters." In school, Marc says his favorite subject is social studies because he likes learning about history. Marc also says that reading isn't his favorite subject, but that "every time I don't like something, I just try and make it better." Through this one statement, Marc shows us that he is willing to act in a way that helps him be successful as a reader. This type of positive attitude and dedication is what keeps students engaged in reading. And when they are engaged, their reading skills will improve and their reading horizons will expand.

Being a dedicated reader doesn't mean that Marc won't experience bumps in the road. But they won't stop him. Even in the face of a passage that isn't interesting or that is difficult, Marc will go on and try again. Students who believe that they are successful readers—or are becoming so—are more likely to persevere when reading gets difficult and may even challenge themselves to read harder or longer texts. Dedication can be developed and is an important attribute when learning to decode. You can help students develop dedication.

The Place for Assessment

Students come to Kindergarten and Grade 1 with many diverse language experiences—some are reading already, some are ready to read, some are English language learners, some will present with a reading disability, and nearly all will need support with phonemic awareness and phonics. English language learners may or may not have already developed phonemic awareness in another language. We need to start where our students are at and that means using a trusted screening assessment tool. We cannot, however, overlook the importance of teacher knowledge in assessment. Teachers can spot difficulties early and remediate quickly.

Screening assessments: These tests provide an early indication of which students might be at risk for reading difficulties. For younger students, these provide information about phonemic awareness, phonics knowledge, and vocabulary.

Three other forms of assessment have a place in every reading classroom:

Diagnostic assessments: These are tests that give in-depth, detailed diagnostic information about students' progress in the components of reading. They can help you make decisions about instruction for each student.

Formative assessments: These assessments provide ongoing information about students' progress and are tied to specific curriculum. You look for information about what students have learned from your instruction. Benchmarks are used to assess progress.

Summative assessments: These final or outcome assessments are administered at the end of the school year.

The Place for Levelled Assessment Materials

One of the tangential strengths of levelled testing materials is that they often provide background information about teaching reading that can help you grow professionally.

You need to know about students' reading behaviors and competencies and be able to compare those to typical progressions of competencies from childhood to adulthood. Levelled materials for assessment were created to do just that. They indicate students' independent, instructional, and frustration reading levels. By identifying a student's level, you can better decide how to help the student progress. One of the tangential strengths of these assessment materials is that they often provide background information about teaching reading that can help you grow professionally.

But—and this is an important *but*—the levelled testing materials are a *starting point* for instruction. They should be easy and fairly quick to administer so that you can get on with the more important job of teaching!

Key Strategies to Help You Teach Decoding

In the following pages of this chapter, I have gathered both new and familiar instructional strategies and practices from teachers, researchers, and my own experience. You can use them to develop students' decoding skills while remembering to keep instruction fun, relaxed, and enjoyable. These seven strategies highlight decoding but also build capacity in the other components of reading—including fluency, vocabulary, and comprehension.

1. Lead guided reading groups
2. Teach decoding through shared reading
3. Inspire students to be word detectives
4. Put their names in lights
5. Get older students decoding
6. Provide write-to-read activities
7. Choose the right books

1. Lead Guided Reading Groups

Guided reading groups are used frequently throughout elementary schools to provide instruction. The format is pretty standard: small groups of students at about the same level of reading proficiency meet with you every week to read a text together. The goal is to support students in reading the text successfully and fluently using a combination of the reading components: decoding, fluency, vocabulary, and comprehension. Both the students' needs as readers and the text determine what you should focus on and how you would structure the lesson.

Decoding lessons are well suited to small groups of students. You can use these opportunities to observe how well students are making sense of written text. Further, students get the one-on-one attention that they need. Remember that students struggle with decoding in a wide variety of ways. The small-group format allows you to focus on each student's unique challenges.

Generally speaking, students learn decoding more successfully in small groups than when working on their own. Participants tend to be more focused and attentive to the reading. In addition, they do not feel singled out, as they would in a large group.

Guided Reading

Guided reading provides opportunities for
- small-group instruction
- personalizing instruction
- practicing pre-reading strategies such as predicting, examining images, and reviewing unfamiliar vocabulary before reading
- grouping students with similar reading abilities
- providing attention to one or more of the reading components: decoding, fluency, vocabulary, and comprehension

Note: Always have a copy of the text for every reader, and always limit to 15 to 20 minutes of instruction.

Book Clubs and Literature Circles

Guided reading groups continue to be an effective instructional strategy as students progress to upper elementary, middle, and high school. With older students, you might refer to these groups as book clubs or literature circles. Like guided reading groups, they provide small-group instruction and interaction around a specific text.

I suggest two strategies in planning book clubs. First, you must skillfully plan the composition of student groups. You can place readers at similar levels into groups so that they can read texts and together develop the specific skills they need as readers. Second, you choose different books for each book club, but ensure that the books are linked in some way. For instance, if you are a Grade 3 teacher, you might have each book club read a different book by the same author, like Kate DiCamillo. You would make this choice knowing that DiCamillo's books will meet a variety of reading needs. *The Tale of Despereaux* might meet the needs of readers with greater proficiency, while books like *Bink and Gollie* (co-authored with Alison McGhee) will appeal to students who require more support in learning to read.

The benefit of using the same author appears when all the students get together in a large group to talk about their books. All students can contribute to a discussion because their books all have something in common. In this case, it is the author, but you could accomplish the same goal by choosing books with the same theme, setting, or problem. At times, I have observed students wanting to read the books from the other clubs after hearing about them. Sometimes they do so, even when those books are challenging. These types of flexible groupings avoid stigmatizing students as "slower readers" and encourage students to read more challenging texts.

Teachers have told me that they find it helpful to do a novel study at least once with all students early in the school year to show students the process for working together and creating community in reading groups. (You can read more about novel studies in Chapter 4.) In a novel study or in book clubs, you model the process for reading the book and then, over time, give students the following four rotating roles to help them build confidence and interest in reading:

- **Converser**: a member of the group who leads the reading session by reviewing the purpose for reading and by assigning how the chapters will be read (that is, silently, in pairs, or aloud). The converser then leads the discussion, inviting others to participate at the end of the reading.
- **Word finder**: a member of the group who keeps a list of the vocabulary that is unfamiliar or that students ask about during the reading. The word finder then leads a discussion about meanings before, during, or after the reading.
- **Questioner**: a member of the group who writes down questions about the reading based on plot, characters, genre, and setting that arise for the group during the reading. The questioner asks others for their questions and presents them all for discussion at the end of the reading.
- **Summarizer**: a member of the group who gives a synopsis of what has been read and understood. The summarizer also comments on the process followed by the group.

When you first introduce book clubs to your students, you will probably fulfill these roles yourself, to model how students can participate fully as group

Teaching Tip
Early in the school year, do a novel study with the whole class to show students the process for working together and creating community in reading groups.

How to Book Club

Congratulations! You are a member of a book club.
Here are a few things to keep in mind while you read together.

1. Everyone participates.
2. Listen to what others say.
3. Be respectful.
4. Keep your focus on the book.
5. Take notes.

THE CONVERSER leads the discussion, inviting group members to participate at the end of the reading.	**THE WORD FINDER** keeps a list of the vocabulary that is unfamiliar or that group members ask about during the reading.
THE QUESTIONER writes down questions that group members have during the reading.	**THE SUMMARIZER** gives a synopsis of what has been read.

Pembroke Publishers ©2021 *Sometimes Reading Is Hard* by Robin Bright ISBN 978-1-55138-351-4

members. You can thereby show students the routines and protocols they should follow to participate in the club. Eventually, you turn these roles over to your students, depending on their age and needs. You may also wish to take part in and contribute to each group for a while so that you can ensure the groups are operating well and so that you can view the reading process experienced by individual members of the group. A graphic organizer like the one on the next page is helpful to facilitate the process and may be used for a single chapter or an entire book.

High school students may be afraid to talk about reading if they feel it will reveal their weaknesses. For this age group, putting students together according to their perceived challenges has been shown to be successful. It allows you to address students' reading needs appropriately and in a space they find safe and free from judgement.

The level of success of guided reading experiences for adolescents is influenced by three important factors:

- the level of the text being appropriate to the students' reading needs
- the students' understanding of the purpose for reading the text
- the ability of students to link the text to their personal circumstances

When readers are matched appropriately to texts at their reading level for part of the school day, they have a chance to read competently, displaying both interest in and persistence to learn what is being read.

2. Teach Decoding through Shared Reading

Stephen King says, "Of the books I read each year, anywhere from six to a dozen are on tape."

Do you like listening to someone read a story? Many people do. Audiobooks are gaining in popularity, ushering in a new way to consume books. Pew research says that approximately one in five North Americans now listen to audiobooks.

Listening to books on tape is great, but shared reading offers an added benefit: you can provide important targeted instruction that would not be possible if your students were listening to a book on tape.

The strategy of shared book reading is commonly understood to be reading aloud for a specific purpose. Students actively participate in this structured reading experience. Shared book reading can take place in a whole-class setting, whereby all students are able to see the same text, perhaps on a document projector. Shared book reading can also be used effectively with small groups of students, whereby each student has a copy of the book or can see a book that you hold.

Teaching Tip
During a shared reading, you can introduce and reinforce decoding skills before students are expected to apply them in guided or independent reading.

In most cases, you would select a text referred to as a "mentor text," that is, a book that you can use to mentor the development of skills in one or more of the reading components. The mentor text should have a reading level that allows students to read and enjoy the book along with you. At the same time, during the shared reading you can introduce and reinforce literacy skills and strategies such as decoding before students are expected to apply them in guided or independent reading.

Shared book reading is an excellent strategy for teaching and practicing the skills of decoding. One favorite book for beginning readers, *Jamberry* by Bruce Degen, is a great choice to focus students' attention on the letter *b* and the sound /b/ in the many words that appear in this fun book. You might ask students to point a finger at the book each time they hear a word with the /b/ sound. In this way, you can see when phonological awareness needs extra support and when it is starting to take shape. (You will find a sampling of books that lend themselves to lessons on decoding in the next section on mentor texts.)

. . . .

STEP BY STEP: Five Days of Shared Book Reading

Inspired by New Zealand author and educator Jill Eggleton (2015), here is a five-day shared book reading protocol that you can use and modify to meet your needs teaching decoding and reading to students. Each day of five, you use the same engaging book in brief lessons of just 10 to 15 minutes. For this lesson, I suggest you use the book *Hattie and the Fox* by Mem Fox and illustrated by Patricia Mullins for a Grade 1 classroom. You should modify this strategy for your students and grade level.

DAY 1: UNDERSTANDING THE STORY

Begin by choosing an engaging book for reading aloud to students. It should lend itself to a focus on an aspect of phonemic awareness and phonics knowledge that students need. The book should be of interest to the age group of your students and include several of the characteristics of high-quality books for young readers: alliteration, rhythm and rhyme, predictability, repetition, language patterns, and high-frequency words.

Read the entire book aloud, showing the pictures and text and using loads of expression and voice characterizations. There are several animal characters in *Hattie and the Fox*, and each can be given its own unique voice.

Following the reading, focus on students' comprehension of the story by asking questions about meaning.

- Who are the characters in the story?
- What can you tell me about them?
- Where does this story take place?
- What was the problem in the story?

Discussing a book with a partner promotes collaboration for learning to read.

Next, ask students to turn to a partner. Discussion with partners promotes collaboration for learning to read. One student pretends to be a character in the story, such as Hattie the hen. This student tells the second student who they are pretending to be. The second student asks questions.

To illustrate, you might bring a student up to the front and ask them which character from the story they would like to be. The student might say, "Hattie." Then you ask the other students, "What would you like to ask Hattie?" Questions might range from, "Were you scared, Hattie?" to "Why didn't you run away?"

After students participate in this role-playing activity with their partners, bring the class together and invite them to share their questions and responses.

DAY 2: VOCABULARY AND PHRASING

On Day 2, read the story aloud and again ask students to read along this time.

Choose key words and patterns to focus on during the reading. These should include word meanings, pronunciations, and spellings. Using *Hattie and the Fox*, help students read this phrase together, "Goodness, gracious me," with expression and fluency.

Record words that are unusual or unfamiliar on chart paper. Give your list the title "Wow Words." For *Hattie and the Fox*, choose the words *nose, eyes, ears, legs, body,* and *tail*. The students say the words along with you as you record them.

Then ask students what these words have in common. Students may notice that they are all parts of the fox's body. They may also point out that humans have these same body parts, except for the tail!

Suggest that there are a few unfamiliar words and record these on your Wow Words chart: *frightened, flew, nearby*, and *loudly*. Ask students what they know about the meanings of these words and add to their responses to ensure they all understand this new vocabulary.

DAY 3: FLOW AND FLUENCY

Today, tell your students, "We are going to read *Hattie and the Fox*, and this time we are going to look for clues to help us know how to read this story."

Read the story as students read along. Stop to look at punctuation marks and font size, calling them "clues to help readers." In *Hattie and the Fox*, there are question marks, exclamation marks, and quotation marks to examine. In each instance, help students identify the marks and consider their usefulness. For instance,

- Point to the sentence, "Good grief," and ask students if they can identify the marks around these two words. Someone says, "Speech marks."
- Reinforce the idea that speech marks tell you that someone in the story is talking. Ask, "Who is speaking here?"

Continue seeking clues with students to help them read the story. As the clues are found, circle them using a pointer or have students come up and do the same.

DAY 4: PHONEMIC AWARENESS AND PHONICS KNOWLEDGE

Begin by reviewing with students the previous days' readings and again ask students to read the story with you. This time, focus on letter knowledge and sounds.

Point to the repeated phrase, "Goodness, gracious me," and indicate that the first two words start with the letter *g* and the hard /g/ sound. Ask students to clap the syllables while they repeat the phrase.

Write the word *goodness* on chart paper and ask students if they see a word within the word. Likely, a student will call out, "good." Point out that the word *good* is on the word wall and ask a student to point to it. Then, turning back to the book, cover up the word *good* so that students can only see the syllable *-ness*. Ask students to say it a few times, and then read the whole word together. Tell students that this word is made up of two parts.

If there are words in the story that lend themselves to exploration of onsets and rimes, commonly referred to in classrooms as "word families," you might choose one or two to focus on. In the story, *Hattie and the Fox*, for example, you might choose the word *sheep* and ask students to tell you what a sheep looks like (you can have an image ready to share) before asking them to help you create a word family chart for _eep. Record words as students brainstorm words that rhyme with *sheep*:

- sheep
- beep
- keep
- deep
- sleep
- weep
- steep
- jeep
- peep

When a student suggests the word *leap* (and someone will), write the word in a second column. Tell students that leap is part of a new word family because it is spelled with *ea* in the middle instead of *ee* as in the other words they have brainstormed.

You say, "Now you know how to read the word *sheep*, and any other words in this word family!"

(*Note:* I suggest exploring just one or two word families per book. This will further students' reading skills without overwhelming them or taking away from the meaning of the text.)

Word Family Display for Grades 2 and 3			
Word Families List 1			
_at	_an	_ap	_ad
	pan		bad
	man		dad
	fan	cap	fad
cat	Dan	map	had
bat	can	rap	lad
sat	ban	tap	mad
hat	ran	sap	pad
rat	tan	gap	dad
mat	van	lap	tad
fat	plan	nap	glad
at		zap	
pat		clap	
flat			

This word family display would be suitable for Grades 2 or 3.

DAY 5: ORAL AND WRITTEN RESPONSE

Students work in pairs or small groups to respond to the story in a variety of ways. Organize students to participate in one or more of the following response activities:

- guided reading groups
- story retelling through drama
- a written or visual response (or a combination of the two)

· ·

Shared book reading is a key practice for supporting students' reading and decoding skills. To maintain students' enthusiasm and interest in reading, use high-quality, engaging literature that appeals to students. This five-day protocol demonstrates one way to teach the skills of decoding while keeping students interested in the text. You can also use non-fiction texts and poetry for this practice to appeal to students who want to read about specific topics.

Mentor Texts for Shared Book Reading

Books for a shared book reading should be chosen to help develop specific reading skills. The books selected are often referred to as "mentor texts" because

A mentor text is a book that you use to mentor development of the skills in one or more of the reading components.

you can use them to mentor the development of skills in one or more of the reading components. The books vary in content, and they can be both fiction and non-fiction.

Choosing Mentor Texts to Develop Phonemic Awareness

Select books, poems, or songs that contain rhyming words, focus on specific sounds, and have a fun or silliness factor. Consider books that let you stress the sounds of language and s-t-r-e-t-c-h out words. A few examples:

- *Sheep in a Jeep* by Nancy Shaw
- *Did You Take the B from My _ook?* by Beck and Matt Stanton
- *Is Your Mama a Llama?* by Deborah Guarino
- *Rhyming Dust Bunnies* by Jan Thomas

Choosing Mentor Texts to Develop Phonics Knowledge

Select books that introduce and reinforce phonics knowledge in an explicit manner, specifically for high-utility phonics skills.

In addition, consider books that do more—books that expand cultural understanding, stimulate imagination, develop critical thinking, or simply encourage talk. A few examples:

- *The Magic of Letters* by Tony Johnston
- *If the S in Moose Comes Loose* by Peter Hermann
- *P is for Pterodactyl: The Worst Alphabet Book Ever* by Raj Haldar and Chris Carpenter
- *Did You Eat the Parakeet?* by Mark Iacolina

In Anna's Classroom: Decoding Fun with Reading

Kindergarten teacher Anna led her students in an enthusiastic shared reading activity to teach decoding using the book *Llama Llama Red Pajama* by Anna Dewdney. For her spellbound audience of five-year-olds, Anna addressed phonemic awareness by having students fill in missing rhyming words while they read the story with her. She focused especially on the words *pajama* and *mama*.

She stopped after reading the sentence, "Baby Llama starts to fret," and asked students to say and s-t-r-e-t-c-h the word *fret* with her. She then asked, "What does *fret* mean?" Students came up with the synonym *worry*, and Anna nodded in agreement. She asked students to show what fret looked like on their faces. Lots of frowning and worried looks ensued.

Moving on to developing phonics knowledge, Anna asked, "What letter does *fret* start with?" A student quickly answered, "*f*." Anna followed up by asking "Does anyone in the classroom have a name that starts with the letter *f*?" As one would expect, Fernando smiled and said, "That's me."

Anna continued: "Let's see how many sounds are in the word *fret*. Put up one finger for each sound you hear." Anna had the students sound out the word *fret* again in an exaggerated way as she watched them put up a finger for each new sound they said and heard.

In little more than a few minutes, Anna had successfully focused on decoding with her students, emphasizing phonemic awareness and phonics knowledge, while engaging them in a fun, interactive read-aloud session with a wonderful book.

3. Inspire Students to Be Word Detectives

To help students move from the oral work of phonemic awareness to the print work of phonics, it helps to inspire students to see themselves as word detectives. For our uses, a word detective is someone interested in using letter-sound associations to figure out new words. When a word detective reads, they

- look for syllables
- look for sight words
- look at the beginning and the end of the word
- look for parts of the word
- look for words inside the word

. . . .

STEP BY STEP: Let's Practice Being Word Detectives

You can have fun dressing up for this lesson. Many students will have no trouble recognizing you as a detective if you don a costume based on Sherlock Holmes. Wearing a special hat and carrying a magnifying glass is a must!

Begin the lesson by saying, "Today we are going to read a story together, and then we are going to be detectives to see what we can find out about the words in this story."

Discuss the word *detective*. Write the word *detective* on the whiteboard. Together with students, say the word, clap the syllables, name the letters, and sound out the word while pointing to each letter. Later, place a card with the word on the word wall.

Students should connect the word *detective* with the action of looking carefully at something to learn new information. Review how magnifying glasses can help this process.

First reading. For this lesson, you might use the book, *Sheep in a Jeep* by Nancy Shaw. This is a favorite of students in the early grades. Read the story expressively as a shared read-aloud, focusing on the humorous story line and the wonderful artwork. This step lets students see that reading starts with a meaningful story. Emphasize the rhyming words and exaggerate the /E/ sound in many of the words, such as *jeep, sheep, dear, cheer*, and *sweep*. At this stage, many students will chime in on the rhyming words, a practice that you should encourage.

Discuss letter *e*. Before the second reading, create a chart with an *e* at the top. Say, "Now we are going to be detectives," and take out your magnifying glass. Tell students that many words in the story have the /E/ sound, pronounced like this: "Eeee." Ask students to make the sound and look at their partners to show how the mouth is shaped when making the /E/ sound.

Second reading. On the second reading, pause at specific times and ask students to supply the rhyming words when they appear in the story. Ask students to tell you when there is a word with the /E/ sound so that you can look at it with the magnifying glass and see what letters are used to make that sound.

Record the words the students find in two columns. One column is headed with "ee" and the other with "ea."

ee	ea
beep	leap
sheep	dear
jeep	heap
cheer	cheap
steer	
weep	
sweep	

These are the /E/ words that students might identify in Sheep in a Jeep *by Nancy Shaw.*

Teaching Tip

When you think your students will understand the following reading rule, introduce it: "When two vowels go walking, the first one does the talking." You might want to add the refrain, "but not all of the time!"

Discuss. Tell students that they have been very good detectives by finding the /E/ sound throughout the story. Ask students to read the words in each column, taking time to have them spell each word and raise their fingers to show how many sounds they hear. This helps students to understand that two letters, in this case either *ee* or *ea*, make one sound when they appear together.

Follow up. To follow up, you might use the book *Sheep in a Jeep* during guided reading in small groups to practice reading the words in context, have students engage in a partner game using onsets and rimes to create words with *ee* and *ea* in them, or do a writing activity using words from the chart you created together. You might also have students take a learning centre approach, having students participate in all three of these activities, one by one.

Another good follow-up is to provide students with other great picture books to read and practice their new decoding knowledge about the /E/ sound. Examples include books such as *The Bee Tree* by Patricia Polacco, *Where Is the Green Sheep?* by Mem Fox, *Who Has These Feet?* by Laura Hulbert, and *Peep!* by Maria van Lieshout.

. . . .

What to Do When Sound and Letter Knowledge Just Won't Stick

Some students may need assistance to remember letter sounds, but first you will have to identify those students. Observe students as they choose a book and open it. Look closely at what your students do when they read.

- Do they look at the cover?
- Do they turn pages from right to left?
- Do they track print across the page from left to right?
- Once students begin looking at letters and making sounds, do they point to letters and make their associated sounds?
- Do they blend the sounds together to make a word?

If some of your students are struggling to remember letter sounds, they will need more practice to develop phonological awareness. You may have to set aside time to work with them in small groups or one on one to isolate and teach specific sounds. It is not uncommon for young children to have difficulty pronouncing the /l/ sound in the word *yellow*, making it sound like the /w/ sound. This is quite normal, but as it affects reading and spelling, you should pull out the metaphorical magnifying glass to help the child sort through this difficulty.

- Help the student practice the /l/ sound in front of you, copying your lip and tongue movements.
- Say more words that begin with the /l/ sound.
- Move on to words with the /l/ sound in the middle and at the end of words.

Your efforts should help the student associate the correct sound with the letter *l*.

Raven, one of my pre-service teachers, had a practicum in a Grade 2 classroom. One day she observed a young student during a one-on-one reading session and then posted this message to get some help from the teacher Twitter community:

Teacher friends. Is it normal for an emergent reader to swap letter order? For example, [the reader] read *oven* as "nov" and read *of* as "for." Is this normal or a red flag? I also see the reader can recognize sight words but can't seem to sound out or decode new ones. Help?

With this bit of description, it is possible to begin thinking about how this student is making sense of print. I sent the following email in reply. You will notice that I am using my knowledge about decoding to help the pre-service teacher consider how to help the student.

Dear Raven,

You have made an important observation and now let's talk about how to provide helpful instruction. What the student may be doing is what many young readers do: making a guess based on the first few letters they see. The student is likely relying on sight word knowledge to read at this point. You want to encourage him to decode to make sense of the words he is reading in addition to learning to read on sight.

Students should not only learn to read through sight words (though they certainly do need a repertoire of these) because eventually they need decoding skills as vocabulary gets more complex and difficult. This is one of the most important reasons that we encourage students to be word detectives.

When a word comes up that a student doesn't recognize, it is important to s-t-r-e-t-c-h the word out from beginning to end and sound it out. Give the student a pretend magnifying glass to use on hard words. Some kind of prop is very helpful in teaching strategies like decoding. It signals to the student that they are doing something new or different as readers.

On a sticky note, write *o v e n*. Point to the first letter and sound it out together. The word *oven* is actually a difficult word to do this with because the *o* makes an /u/ sound rather than an /O/ or /o/ sound. You will want to note that with the student. The other example you gave is the word *for*, and this makes me think that the student may struggle with the letter *o* specifically. If so, work on words that have the letter *o* either at the beginning or the middle of words. This will help to build the student's confidence, which will be needed for future decoding.

4. Put Their Names in Lights

Teaching Tip
Students' own names supply some of the most meaningful words for developing phonemic awareness and phonics in the classroom.

"What's in a name? That which we call a rose / By any other name would smell as sweet." Despite the sentiment of these lines, experience tells us that names are important, especially to children. There is a good reason we get to know our students' names on the first day of school. They matter.

Students' own names supply some of the most meaningful words for developing phonemic awareness and phonics in the classroom. Their own names and those of their peers could not be more interesting to students. By using names in instruction, you can help students view themselves as readers who read meaningful words. It's also fun!

Research says that students should be able to look around their classroom and find their names in ten different places. That's right. Ten! You can plaster them everywhere: on a word wall, a coat rack, a boot cubby, a mailbox, a desk or table, a book box, the attendance chart, the student-of-the-week poster, and a list of classroom jobs. Enabling students to look around in a new environment and recognize their own name gives them proof that they belong. Such a practice is valuable for students for both self-esteem and reading success.

....

STEP BY STEP: Get to Know Me

Begin by asking students to stand and form a circle. Tell students, "Today we are going to use our own names to learn about sounds, letters, and words."

Model clapping the syllables of your name. Say, "Let's start with my name." Use your first name or the name you like your students to call you. Introduce the word *syllable* to the students by writing it on the board. Explain that a syllable is a part of a word. Clap the syllables in your name two or three times as you repeat it and then ask your students to join you several times until they accurately clap the number of syllables in your name.

Clap one another's names. Going around the circle one way first and then the other, students clap the syllables in their own and others' names all together. Repeat any names that are not clapped accurately the first time. Students need to be able to identify the syllables in the names to benefit from the next part of the lesson.

Sort by number of syllables. Post signs that say, "My name has 1 clap," "My name has 2 claps," "My name has 3 claps," and "My name has 4 claps." Ask students to line up behind the sign that matches their name. Each row of students claps the syllables in everyone's name, first in their own row and then in all the rows. In this way, students hear their peers' names and associate those with the number of claps and syllables.

Practice with partners. Students then find partners. Each pair practices clapping the syllables in their two names. Then each student finds a new partner to practice with. This continues until everyone has clapped the names of at least four partners.

Recognizing initial letters. Next, draw students' attention to the letters of the alphabet, which you likely have posted around one or two walls of the classroom. Ask students to stand in front of the letter that begins their name. You have now moved students from an oral activity designed to support phonemic awareness to a print activity to develop phonics knowledge. Encourage students to say and clap, one at a time or in pairs, like this: "My name is Robin, and it begins with the letter *R*."

This is a great activity to do in the first week of the school, while students are getting to know one another and you are getting to know them. You can continue developing phonics knowledge on another day using Name Games, described in the next feature.

....

STEP BY STEP: Name Games

Prepare name cards. For every student, prepare a large card with their name printed on it, a capital letter for the first letter and lowercase for the others. There should be a bit of space between the letters, but the name should still be easily recognizable. For instance, here are the name cards for Ben and Angela.

Compare name cards. Pair students so that they can compare their written names and talk about how they are the same and different. Two Grade 2 students comparing their names might come up with the following observations:

- "Ben's name has 3 letters and 1 syllable. Angela's name has 6 letters and 3 syllables."
- They notice that both of them have an *e* somewhere in the middle of their names.
- With your help, they may notice that Ben's name starts and ends with a consonant, while Angela's name starts and ends with a vowel.

Share observations. Once students make their observations, they join another pair and tell them what they learned about their names. You can switch up the groups as often as you like if students are enjoying the game. During this sharing exercise, students are learning to recognize words, letters, sounds, syllables, and the names of their classmates. This type of collaboration is key to keeping students engaged and learning from one another.

Play the name game. Next, ask students to take their cards and cut their names into individual letters.

To begin, students play the name game with their partner. They turn over the letters for both names and mix them up. Then, they pick them up one at a time and try to find the letters to spell both names. When they have done this successfully, the students join another pair, this time playing the same game with four sets of names and letters.

It is not uncommon for students to ask to play this game with even more of their classmates or to continue playing after the recess bell has gone off. I have watched students engaged in phonemic awareness and phonics games that featured their own names for 30 minutes or more with little or no indication of getting bored or tired.

. . . .

5. Get Older Students Decoding

Most of us are not aware that we continue to use our decoding skills in reading as we get older simply because we do it automatically. For example, when I am reading a novel and the name of a character is several syllables long with letters that I rarely see used together, I sometimes take the time to sound the name out so that I can say it in my head as I read. I might even search the name on an app to hear its correct pronunciation.

In this example, I was determined to decode the name so that I could better enjoy reading my novel. I do this for place names, too, like Ballachulish and Fjällbacka. Enabling our students to embrace the same determination to decode words will benefit them through their schooling and into adulthood. As students enter middle and high school, their reading assignments become more complex and disciplinary in nature. They read increasingly in subjects such as social studies, mathematics, science, and the arts. And *learning new vocabulary is at the heart of disciplinary reading.* Unfortunately, as students get older, reading tends to be assigned, yet little time is devoted to reading instruction. Many older students still need to develop the skills of examining, sounding out, spelling, and making sense of unfamiliar words.

Learning new vocabulary is at the heart of disciplinary reading.

The Challenge of Multisyllabic Words

I remember as a child being so proud when I could pronounce the word *supercalifragilisticexpialidocious*, from the film *Mary Poppins*, both forward and backward (*dociousaliexpisticfragicalirupus*). We might not have much need to read words with 14 syllables, but as we develop as readers we all need to be able to decode multisyllabic words.

While many struggling readers at the secondary level are proficient at reading new single-syllable words such as *vibe, fact,* and *cell,* they may lack strategies to decode the multisyllabic words that are common in higher-level reading materials. Often termed "advanced word study," interventions in this area generally include instruction in word recognition and word analysis. If you are engaging in this work, you likely focus on multisyllabic words because these words encompass most of the new vocabulary encountered by adolescents in their reading. Multisyllabic words also provide much of the new information in content-area texts.

Teaching word-analysis strategies for decoding multisyllabic words helps adolescent readers decode unknown words, build a sight-word vocabulary, and spell new words. You can use books clubs, literature circles, and other small-group reading opportunities for this kind of instruction. You can also use teachable moments to integrate word study into meaningful, contextually relevant reading.

It goes without saying that word study facilitates students' understanding of the subject or discipline they are reading about. Teachers of all subjects need to embrace this notion that decoding is what all readers do.

6. Provide Write-to-Read Activities

When I began teaching, many teachers believed that students must learn to read before writing can be attempted. I even remember hearing one of my colleagues saying, "I start the Grade 1s writing in November."

Attitudes have changed. Children are now viewed as writers almost from the first moment they pick up a crayon and scribble across a surface. Unfortunately, some children find walls to be the most attractive places to begin their writing careers! Nonetheless, writing is writing.

Encoding is the term used to describe students using their letter-sound knowledge to write. Encoding uses the same skills needed to learn to read but in a different process. Many early writers scribe with "errors," as my daughter did when she wrote the word *then* as *zen*. These writers are merely revealing to us their developing knowledge of phonics through encoding.

> Many early writers scribe with "errors." These writers are revealing to us their developing knowledge of phonics through encoding.

Make Time for Writing

You can make time for daily writing in your classroom in a variety of ways. All of the following would support decoding.

Set up a writing centre. A writing centre should be an area easily accessed by students. It should contain different colors and sizes of paper and other materials to write on. It should have a variety of writing utensils. Encourage students to write lists, reminders, daily goals, and other messages throughout the day. They can be addressed to you, to classmates, or to someone at home. Card-making materials encourage students to give birthday cards to each other and to mark other special occasions, without needing outside resources to do so.

Make letters and words accessible. Keep sets of letters and high-frequency words in containers that students can bring to their desks. These can be letters or words on individual laminated cards, magnetic letters, or letters on blocks. When students are writing, they can use the letters to spell out words, which they can, in turn, copy onto a page. Having the opportunity to move letters around to spell words before writing them on a page is an effective aid for learning how to decode and encode.

Writing during play. Encourage students to integrate writing experiences into their play. This can be as simple as adding writing materials to the places where students play. For instance, if you have a building centre in Kindergarten with blocks, hard hats, and other building materials, include a book called "Class Blueprints," where students can draw and label what they build.

"Who Are You?" Stories

When students write about themselves, their families, and other personal experiences, they show what they know about written language.

Give them a reason to write. Begin by telling your students that they are going to interview you. Explain that they can ask any question they like, and that you will answer them. Request that they take notes of the answers you give, so that they can remember what you said. Tell them that they can use pictures, letters, or words to record your responses.

The interview. It is likely students will eagerly pepper you with questions like, "Do you have any pets?" "What hobbies do you have?" "What is your favorite food?" And of course, their favorite, "How old are you?"

After you answer each question, ask the student who posed it, "What could you write down to help you remember my answer?" You might stop and write a word on the board to help students learn, or practice writing, a particular word. This provides an opportunity to teach specific decoding skills that you are working on.

Eventually, every student should have something written about you on a piece of paper.

A sharing session. Have students read back what they wrote in a sharing session. As they do this, you can provide decoding instruction as "one piece of advice" for each student. The decoding advice you provide might be as simple as writing a simple consonant-vowel-consonant (c-v-c) word like *dog* to represent a drawing they created. Your more capable students might require a different kind of advice, such as a suggestion to use capital letters at the beginning of sentences.

Wrap-up. Ask students to create a portrait of you by drawing a picture and adding information they learned about you from their interview sheets. Together, you can create a bulletin board display called, "Our Teacher."

Date stamp the students' pages, especially if this activity is done early in the year. Then repeat it a few months later to see writing and decoding progress. (You can also learn a lot about how your students see you through their drawings!)

Inventive Spelling

Once children have been exposed to letters and sounds, their writing reflects their new knowledge. In a sense, watching students write gives you a window into how they are reading.

It is exciting when students begin to recognize that sounds and letters go together in print. As might be expected, beginning consonants are easiest to recognize and these may be what you see first, as they are sometimes used to represent an entire word. Later, final consonants are added and, later still, middle consonants and vowels.

The best way to develop phonemic awareness, the precursor to spelling, is through invented spelling; children with pens, pencils, crayons, drawing, and writing.
—Marilyn Adams, *Beginning to Read: Thinking and Learning About Print*, 1994

This process is sometimes referred to as "the reinvention of language" because it looks as if students are inventing the spellings of words as they write. Students' "inventive spelling" lets you glimpse into the student's mind to see how they are making sense of the sounds and letters as they learn to read and write. Students need assurances and support at this stage. They cannot be spontaneous in their writing if they learn to constantly check with you to see if they are doing it right.

As children continue to write with confidence, their words evolve into what many teachers call "the standard version." For example, *luv* becomes *love*, *wont* becomes *want*, and *iz* becomes *is*. This can be a long stage for some students. It is not uncommon for some students to be using inventive spelling for some words well into fifth grade, especially with words that we wouldn't expect students to be able to spell at that age. I can't tell you how many times I saw the word *they* spelled as *thay* in Grade 4. Eventually, though, all my students learned to use the standard version consistently. One of my favorite inventive spellings was a Grade 4 student's version of *all of a sudden*, which he spelled as *allasuden*. Admit it, it does sound like one word sometimes.

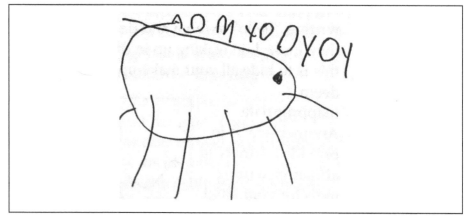

A Kindergartener draws a picture and then prints the letters he hears in his name (Adam), before adding more letters to tell a story.

7. Choose the Right Books

We know that when students read what interests them, even if it is challenging, they will stick with it. A combination of 1) reading challenge and 2) reading interest builds confidence and dedication for reading. Choosing the right books involves making sure your students have access to two types of reading material:

1. books and texts they can read independently (with 90–95 percent accuracy), so they can experience success
2. books and texts they choose for themselves for enjoyment. These can be texts that you might consider above their reading level and that is okay. New research tells us that when students are interested in what they read, they are motivated to meet the challenge of harder text.

Both types of books are important to readers. Books at students' independent reading levels will address negative thinking like, "I am not going to read this because it is too hard." Statements like this lead to thoughts like, "I think reading is a waste of time" or "I try to get out of reading books for school." This is reading avoidance and, unfortunately, it develops in far too many students. Addressing students' thoughts about reading and choosing the right books to develop their reading skills can help. You can read more on how to combat negative thinking about reading in Chapter 4.

Just-Right Texts

Your challenge is to find just-right books for every individual student.

When students are beginning their reading lives, we want to use the Goldilocks principle to match readers to texts that are neither too hard nor too easy, but just right for the reader. Your challenge is to find just-right books for every individual student. These are books that students can read and therefore want to read. They also provide enough of a challenge that students can improve their reading skills.

Have you noticed how some students gravitate toward fiction while others turn to non-fiction when making their own choices about what to read? Observations like these are important. Typically, many teachers rely heavily on using fiction for beginning readers, but not all students are interested in that genre. You may lose young readers because the texts you provide do not interest them. That can be fixed.

Many decodable books offer stilted and unnatural language. These can be used in the early stages of learning to read, but you should watch for signs of students losing interest in these texts. Choices should always be guided by what students need—and if they need engaging, fun, beautifully written books, you should make sure they get them.

Here are some classic books you can use to teach decoding:

- the Chicka Chicka Boom Boom series by Bill Martin, Jr., and John Archambault
- the Brown Bear, Brown Bear, What Do You See? series written by Bill Martin, Jr., and Eric Carle
- *Go, Dog, Go!* by P. D. Eastman
- *Hop on Pop* and *The Foot Book* by Dr. Seuss

Above-Level Books

Early in my teaching career, I learned that when students start to lose interest in the reading in class, you need to take action. Observing and talking to the student and family or caregivers is essential. When you pinpoint the reason for the loss of interest, you can pivot your instruction and modify or change the text to ensure it is meaningful to the student.

Sometimes a child is drawn to a book that is far too challenging for their current ability. Instead of redirecting the child, you may see an opportunity to channel the interest this book provides.

In My Classroom: Aaron's Story

I'd like to tell you about a former student of mine: Aaron. His story shows how you can take action to transform a lack of interest into avid interest.

In one of my first few years of teaching Grade 1, I was using the basal reading series provided to me by the school. It clearly had limited interest for some of my students. I boosted the program with more interesting stories, but after several months, one of my students was still not progressing. Sometimes, he seemed to shut down in language arts class. He would complete his work but without his usual energy.

While chatting with his mom, I discovered that he had a favorite book at home called *The Golden Egg Book* by Margaret Wise Brown. The illustrations are beautiful in this 1947 edition, and the language is lovely. This is probably why Aaron loved it so much.

I asked Aaron to bring the book to school so that we could share it with the class. I told him that I could teach him how to read it. He was excited!

Each page of the book had a lot of print, especially for a beginning reader. In addition, the vocabulary was more difficult than what a student in Grade 1 would be expected to read. It was the kind of book that I would have loved reading aloud to my students for enjoyment, and to practice summarizing or prediction. But it was not a book that I would have chosen to teach reading to a beginner. Aaron had made it abundantly clear, however, that he wanted to learn how to read THIS book.

I undertook to involve Aaron fully in the book. It was important to provide opportunities for him to practice all the components of reading—phonics, phonemic awareness, comprehension, vocabulary, and fluency—using this book.

So together we began to make some shorter books that Aaron helped to write. They all contained aspects from the story line. These "little books," as we called them, also contained vocabulary from the original book but in new formats that could be decoded and read more easily. These formats limited the vocabulary on each page. They also contained some predictable and repetitive sentence patterns, but they still told an interesting part of the story.

The cloze technique omits words from a passage so that readers must use what they know to fill in the blanks.

One of our little books included all the characters and places in the book. Using a cloze technique for the first few pages, Aaron filled in the words that were missing, using the original book as his guide. By the time we were part way through creating the little book, Aaron was writing the sentences himself using his phonics and sight word knowledge. He chose to illustrate his book as well. Aaron proudly read this book during the school day and took it home to read to his parents, all the while developing his reading skills so that he would be able to read *The Golden Egg Book*, which he loved and of course wanted to read on his own.

These pages from Aaron's little book listed the characters in The Golden Egg Book.

These pages from Aaron's little book put two of the characters together in sentences.

In science class, we were already working on learning what are commonly referred to as the *w* words—words such as *who, what, where, when*, and *why*. They appeared on the word wall as well as on a class bulletin board. This was helpful, as the words *what* and *where* appeared in Aaron's book. He learned these words so he could read them in *The Golden Egg Book*, but now he knew them for science class, too.

Using *The Golden Egg Book*, we worked on all the components of reading including decoding, vocabulary, comprehension, and fluency. It was necessary to focus on Aaron's ability to

- enjoy listening to and talking about this story to understand that print carries a message
- identify letters and letter-sound relationships
- write (and then read) words using his phonics knowledge
- read (and then write) high-frequency sight words

I noted that there were several words in *The Golden Egg Book* that contained onsets and rimes that would not only help Aaron read the vocabulary in this book but would give him agency over other words. The words I chose to focus on and that were appropriate for Grade 1 were

- *p – ick*
- *p – eck*
- *cr – ack*
- *h – ill*
- *r – ock*
- *w – ould* (The words *would, could*, and *should* appear in the story.)

I asked Aaron to put these words into his Word Families Book of onsets and rimes, and then he added more words whenever he found others that rhymed with one of the words from *The Golden Egg Book*. In this way, Aaron expanded his knowledge of vocabulary from the book and used his decoding skills to learn many new words that he would encounter in other texts

High-Quality, Engaging Literature

Few students are like Aaron, having one favorite book they want to learn to read. Most students respond to wonderful books of many stripes. So, one of the best ways to provide explicit instruction in decoding while maintaining students' interest in reading is to introduce and use exemplary literature that engages, engrosses, and delights readers but that also provides opportunities to develop students' reading skills.

Fortunately, we have never had so many diverse texts available for readers of all ages that meet both students' skill levels and their interests. My colleague Rhona Harkness tells her pre-service teachers that there is a picture book for every topic, situation, and outcome we teach! (You can find out more about picture books in Chapter 5.)

Engaging books, nursery rhymes, and tongue twisters that have a variety of language features are perfect for developing the skills of phonemic awareness, phonics knowledge, and decoding.

For older readers, any book offers opportunities to teach about language and decoding. The key is to get students into the frame of mind to "do something"

Teaching Tip

Here is what to look for in high-quality, engaging literature for young readers who are developing phonemic awareness and phonics knowledge:
- alliteration
- rhythm and rhyme
- predictability
- repetition
- language patterns
- a mix of high-frequency and juicy words
- words and illustrations that work together to support the story line
- books that create an emotional response in the reader

when they encounter words that they don't know or sections of a text that they don't understand. (We will explore strategies for dealing with new vocabulary in Chapter 4.)

Teaching Tip: *Sources for Book Ideas*

If you are uncertain where to find new texts to use in teaching, it's not too hard to find advice. Talk to your school or public librarian, consult with colleagues, or search online for recently published and reviewed books. Readers' advisory tools are another valuable option. You can use one to find high-quality, age-appropriate books to use in your classroom. A few readers' advisory tools you can find online include Book Riot, Epic, the Canadian Children's Book Centre, NoveList K-8 Plus, Guys Read, and YALSA Excellence in Non-Fiction for Young Adults.

Your Key Takeaways

Here are the key ideas we explored in this chapter on teaching decoding.

- Decoding is a skill that students use based on phonemic awareness, phonics knowledge, and other clues to help them sound out, recognize, and correctly pronounce words.
- The foundations of learning to read are the essential skills of phonemic awareness and phonics knowledge.
- These foundational skills need to be taught playfully, avoiding the drudgery of skill-and-drill methods.
- With young students, it is useful to follow a systematic phonics program linked to literature.
- Students need to learn how to sound out new and unfamiliar words and be able to recognize sight words quickly and automatically.
- Students develop the motivation to read when they can confidently decode print. They work to decode print when they are motivated to read.
- Providing high-quality, engaging literature that students are interested in reading helps them develop the motivation needed to persevere when reading is hard.
- Older students need decoding skills to help them when disciplinary reading becomes more challenging.
- Writing supports students in developing their decoding skills.

3

Fluency: Teaching How to Recognize Words Automatically

Fluency is a wonderful bridge [from decoding] to comprehension and to a life-long love of reading.

—*Maryanne Wolf,* Tales of Literacy for the 21st Century, *2016*

When I was a child, being read to was like being wrapped up in a warm blanket.

I grew up in a household where books, newspapers, and magazines were plentiful. My parents loved to read, and they read aloud often to their five children. "Listen to this…" and "Let me just read you something" were phrases commonly uttered by my parents. When they read aloud, especially my Dad, it was often with great fanfare and exaggerated expression, exact phrasing, and emphasis on particular words for maximum effect on their young listeners. Being read to was like being wrapped up in a warm blanket.

Having our parents model the qualities of fluent reading was critical to our reading development. Our parents also listened to me and my siblings read aloud when we were learning to read. I still remember seeing my younger siblings sitting at the counter in the kitchen with their readers open, pointing to each word. As the big sister listening in, it reminded me of a train chugging up a mountain, slow at first and then cresting the top and picking up speed as it cruised down the mountain. Our mom listened across the room and came over to help when someone paused or seemed to struggle. It was a pressure-free household.

Through these experiences, my siblings and I knew how reading was supposed to sound, that is, a lot like speech: natural, fluid, and full of expression. In other words, we had a model of fluency. You may have had similar experiences. Keep in mind that not all children have such models at home. So you can step in to be that model for them.

What Is Reading Fluency?

As a child, I learned what fluency sounded like. But what exactly is fluency? Language experts describe it as a developmental process that involves automatic recognition of letters, words, and connected text. Fluency is "the ability to read text rapidly, smoothly, effortlessly, and automatically with little attention to the mechanics of reading such as decoding" (Meyer, 1999, p. 284).

Researcher Gene Mehigan (2020) studied the effects of fluency instruction on motivation for reading and concluded that, "The extent to which [students] are motivated by their *early* reading instruction ... has a significant impact on the likelihood of them succeeding in reading, which in turn can impact their school experiences in later years" (p. 2). It is this impact that we must keep in mind as we examine if our reading instruction addresses fluency.

Fluent readers can instantly recognize many words, often referred to as "sight words." When students recognize words quickly, they spend less cognitive energy on decoding text and more on comprehending it. Think about this: Who will get the most reading practice in a ten-minute period: a student who is able to read 200 words fluently in that time or the student who reads just 50 words in the same space of time?

The impact of fluency over time is cumulative. Throughout their whole schooling, fluent readers will continue to read more—and become even more fluent—than non-fluent readers. The difference in sheer volume of material read will have a significant impact on students' reading development and long-term prospects. William James, an early American psychologist, may have said it best when he declared that children who learn to read fluently are taking flight into a whole new world.

The challenge is not small. Students must develop their interest, dedication, and confidence to move from reading one word at a time to reading that emulates the rhythm and ease of speech.

Identifying Fluency Level

Timothy Shanahan offers these three pieces of advice to teachers who want to get a fair assessment of students' level of fluency.

1. Ask students to read a passage as well as they can, not as fast as they can.
2. Let students know that you will talk about the text together after they have read it, a signal that they should read for understanding.
3. Listen to the students read. Ask yourself how close it sounds to speech. (2020)

What Fluency Looks Like

If you are unsure what it means to read fluently, here is what to watch for in your students when they are reading.

When reading is fluent:
- The reader reads at a moderate rate that emulates speech, and with accuracy and expression.
- The reader can focus on comprehending what they read.
- The reader is interested in what they are reading and wants to continue reading.

When reading is not fluent:
- The reader reads very slowly, makes reading errors, and does not use expression.
- The reader has difficulty focusing on the meaning of the text or recalling details and information that has been read.
- The reader loses interest in reading and does not want to continue reading.

Reading Fluency: More than Speed

You may have noticed that the definition I provided at the beginning of the chapter did not mention speed of reading. Accuracy and expression matter as much or more. One mistake some teachers make is teaching fluency in isolation. The trend to think of fluency as distinct from decoding, vocabulary, and comprehension has led to some questionable assessment practices that assess fluency by measuring reading speed.

One of these practices is the timed, repeated reading test. Teachers ask students to read a passage from a text that the student can read with at least 90 to 95 percent accuracy. Teachers often start with a grade-level text and then move up or down depending on the students' ability to read the text with a high degree of accuracy. Then, the teacher times the reading with a stopwatch and calculates the number of words read correctly. Teachers and students repeat this process several times. The teachers then graph the results to demonstrate that, with repeated readings, the students' speed of reading improves.

The problem with this practice is that no consideration is given to how well students comprehend what they read. If students cannot understand what they have read, what is the good of it? Fluency should be discussed and encouraged but never taught or measured in isolation from the other components.

> If students cannot understand what they have read, what is the good of it?

Joseph: A Slow but Fluent Reader

Timed reading tests have often caused teachers and parents to scratch their heads in wonder and ask, "Why is it necessary to time the speed at which a student reads?" Recently, one of my pre-service teachers who is also the dad of a seven-year-old, Joseph, asked me that very question. Joseph's teacher said that, based on timed reading tests, Joseph had problems with reading fluency that needed to be addressed. The teacher told Joseph's dad that he should have Joseph read a single passage four to five times each night. So that is what they did.

Joseph grew bored immediately. To prove to his son the effectiveness of the technique, Joseph's dad thought he would demonstrate that repeated reading was helping Joseph understand the text. After the first, rather slow reading, Joseph's dad asked what the passage was about. To his surprise, Joseph knew exactly what he had read. Not only did he summarize what he read, he provided many details as well. So, Joseph was not reading slowly because he had to decode every word. He was reading at the rate that was necessary for him to *comprehend* what he read.

We all do this as readers. When you read a book for pleasure, you read at the rate you need to help you to understand what you are reading. You slow down when you need to if you come to a passage with a lot of information that you need to digest. You speed up when you are easily understanding everything that you're reading.

All readers should read at the speed that helps them best absorb meaning. Speed, therefore, should never be the goal in and of itself. Joseph did not have a reading problem. The goal of reading instruction should not be on supporting fluency for speed's sake, but so that students can easily comprehend what they read.

Teaching Tip

On the matter of fluency, Marie Clay has this to say, "[R]eading speed and reading fluency are linked to increasing improvement of reading test scores in older readers ... But this does not mean that trying to be a fast reader will make you successful ... Reading successfully enables the reader to become a fast reader!" (2016, pp. 121–122)

Target the Reasons Fluency Is Hard to Achieve

What should you do when students struggle with fluency? I am sure you have watched patiently as students labor over reading, making the sounds of each and every letter until the word finally seems to magically appear before their eyes. Naturally, some of this is normal.

When fluency doesn't improve, however, or if students become discouraged, you have to do something. The first logical step is to identify the underlying reasons for the struggle. You might ask, "Is the lack of fluency related to problems with decoding?" Often, it is.

If there are decoding issues, deal with them first. If you don't, you will see a snowball effect, as students fall further and further behind their classmates.

You may also notice that some students have difficulty picking up on word families. That is, they do not easily recognize how onsets and rimes can pair up, so they cannot apply that knowledge to future reading. For example, they may not easily match onsets such as /k/, /f/, /j/, and /l/ to the rime /ake/ to help them read new words they encounter such as *cake, fake, Jake,* and *lake.* Some students simply need more practice recognizing the word families to improve their fluency.

For other students, fluency remains out of reach because they do not have a repertoire of sight words. In that case, strategies are needed to help students recognize sight words quickly and easily while reading. Having a classroom word wall with common sight words is one strategy.

Teaching Tip: *Pinpointing Barriers to Fluency*

If a student cannot improve their fluency, look backward and forward to pinpoint where the student's difficulties lie. Does the lack of fluency stem from …
- … the student's oral language development?
- … the development of the student's phonemic awareness?
- … the student's phonics and decoding knowledge?
- … the number of sight words the student recognizes automatically?
- … the student's comprehension of the text?

A Common Roadblock to Fluency: Lack of Confidence

Ten-year-old Sydney told me about her progress with reading: "When I started school, I couldn't read but everyone else could. It wasn't fun. Now I can read. I love it." It inspires me to hear kids talk about reading this way. It reminds me of Nancy Frey saying we want students to be able to experience "the skill, will, and thrill" of reading.

On the one hand, when students are self-confident readers, they persevere with reading tasks. They don't give up. When students do not give up, they can enjoy the thrill of reading. On the other hand, when students have reading difficulties early on and they begin to see themselves as "slow" readers, their lack of self-confidence can hobble their efforts to become fluent readers. They do not

A child who feels they are an able and competent reader will be more likely to read and persevere with a challenging text, whereas a child who feels they are unable or lacking in ability will be more likely to avoid the reading activity… Clearly, therefore, it is crucial to develop both positive attitudes to reading and reading confidence at a young age.
—Sarah McGeown, Rhona Johnston, Jo Walker, Kathryn Howatson, Ann Stockburn, and Paul Dufton (2015)

Teaching Tip
Let them know that you are
confident that they will learn to read
fluently.

persevere with reading tasks. Many give up. And then they never enjoy the thrill of reading.

By building up students' confidence levels—by letting them know that *you* are confident that they will learn to read fluently—you might well remove a road-block holding them back.

Identifying students who lack self-confidence is key. If you bring your ability as a "kid-watcher" to the task, it will not take you long to become aware of students' attitudes toward reading and their reading proficiency, even without formal testing. Observe your students and ask them these questions:

- Is reading easy for you?
- Do you think of yourself as a good reader?
- Are you an enthusiastic reader?
- Are you a confident reader?
- Do you find reading hard sometimes?
- What is hard about reading sometimes?
- Do you like reading for pleasure? Are you unenthusiastic about reading for pleasure? Somewhere in the middle?
- What do you think of yourself as a reader?

The answers to these questions will help you to develop each student's reading profile as a starting point in the school year. Resist the temptation to compare one student with another. Each student is on their own unique path toward learning to read.

In Henry's Classroom: Fluency Breeds Confidence

Henry, age nine, is already a fluent, confident reader. When asked if he likes to read, he smiles and his eyes get big when he answers enthusiastically, "Yes! A lot." He says he likes to read fantasy, sorcery, mystery, suspense, and funny stuff. Henry also says his favorite subject is social studies because he likes to read about history.

Henry sees himself as a reader. He reads books on his own so he can learn more about his favorite subject. Given the list of the types of books Henry reads, he also appears to be a skilled and fluent reader. This is not an accident. When students experience success, even at a young age, they tend to read more. This in turn increases their skill and fluency and their positive feelings about reading. How does a student like Henry develop self-confidence as a reader? Like all students, Henry's confidence develops in relation to his reading skills. Self-confidence and the belief in oneself as a reader begins early.

What Doesn't Work: Round Robin Reading

Picture this: A teacher calls on students one at a time to read aloud a section of text. The rest of the students sit quietly and listen (if the teacher is lucky). One student reads aloud while 28 or more other students do … what? Some follow along and others do not. Some students are bored and stare out the window. Others are nervous, awaiting their turns.

Who does not remember taking turns reading aloud in school? I personally loved reading aloud at home while my parents listened, but as soon as I had to read aloud in front of the class, I got incredibly nervous. To this day, I recall repeating the phrase in my head, "Please don't call on me!" whenever the teacher was about to ask students to read aloud. Hardly meaningful reading practice.

One of the drawbacks of students reading aloud one at a time in front of their peers is that it provides little time for actual reading practice. In a class of 25, each student would have just 1 minute of practice in a 25-minute class.

No evidence shows that this round-robin reading strategy—sometimes referred to as popcorn, popsicle stick, touch-and-go, or wraparound reading—improves fluency. The real value of the round-robin lies in how the teacher can use it to control a group of students—not exactly a worthy purpose. As studies show, neither is silent reading the best use of classroom time for students who are just beginning to develop their fluency skills (Hasbrouck, 2006).

We do know that reading aloud helps in developing fluency. According to literacy experts, the only time that one person should be reading aloud to the whole class is when the teacher models reading. Reading aloud can also take place in small groups, with the teacher, or when students are reading on their own. Just not in front of the whole class.

You probably know that, for many students, reading aloud in front of the class is nothing but a painful experience. It is time to put this practice to rest and search out new and more effective ways to support the reading practice needed to develop fluency. You may wish to check out the many read-aloud alternative strategies for students later in this chapter.

What Does Work: Teachers Reading Aloud to Students

Reading aloud to improve fluency and comprehension has a long history in classrooms. At first, it developed because of book scarcity. If there was only one book available, only one person could read at a time. Often it was the teacher who led the reading.

I want to point out that teachers who read aloud to their students are, according to experts, engaging in a greatly beneficial activity. If you already do read aloud to your students, keep it up. If you have let this practice slip away or haven't used it yet, it's time to make it part of your teaching repertoire.

Here are just a few of the benefits of teachers reading aloud to their students:

- improving fluency and comprehension
- modelling fluency by reading at an appropriate pace, with expression and attention to punctuation
- building a reading community
- introducing and teaching new vocabulary
- motivating readers to want to read
- teaching good listening skills

Hints for Improving Your Readings

Practice makes perfect. Reading aloud takes a bit of practice to get it right.
- Read in front of a mirror to see if your facial expressions match the text.
- Record yourself reading aloud and listen to it. What do you notice?
- How is the rate or pace at which you read? Is it too fast or too slow for an interested listener?
- Read aloud to a trusted friend and ask for feedback about your reading voice.

The real value of the round-robin lies in how the teacher can use it to control a group of students—not exactly a worthy purpose.

Tend to what students see. Decide how best to ensure that students can clearly see the text and images as you read.

- Is the book large enough for everyone to see?
- Would a document projector help students to view the text while you read?

Read with expression. Even the most self-conscious of us can "bring it" when reading aloud to our students.

- Are you being sensitive to the mood and how it changes over the course of the story?
- Do you speak in a unique voice for each character?

Choose books that both suit and stretch your audience. Read books aloud that you know will interest your students.

- Do you embrace books that are funny, or gross, or silly, or revolting (within reason!)? These are often very engaging.
- Do you embrace books that might make you and your students emotional? (A little emotion is valuable—these types of books often connect readers to books and to others.)

Teacher's Tip

Always preview books before reading them to your students, to ensure that they are suitable choices.

Refresh Your Reading Aloud Practice with these Books

"Bring the silly" books

- *Splat!* by Jon Burgerman (ages 3–5)
- *Shark vs. Train* by Chris Barton (ages 5–8)
- *The Legend of Rock Paper Scissors* by Drew Daywalt (ages 6–9)
- *Dog Diaries: A Middle School Story* by James Patterson (ages 7-12)
- Phoebe and Her Unicorn series by Dana Simpson (ages 7–14)

"Awesomely gross" books

- *Everyone Poops* by Taro Gomi (ages 3–5)
- *Hobgoblin and the Seven Stinkers of Rancidia* by Kyle Sullivan (ages 8–12)
- *The Finger and the Nose* by Paula Merlan Gomez (ages 4–9)
- *Gross as a Snot Otter* by Jess Keating (ages 5–8)
- *Grossology* by Sylvia Branzei (ages 11–14)

"All the feels" books

- *A Different Pond* by Bao Phi (ages 6–8)
- *Maybe Something Beautiful* by F. Isabel Campoy (ages 4–7)
- *Powwow* by Karen Pheasant-Neganigwane (ages 9–12)
- *Be Kind* by Pat Zietlow Miller (ages 3–6)
- *Small Things* by Mel Tregonning (ages 8–12)

Get Them Reading: Offer Books Tailored to Students' Interests or Just Plain Good Books

Interest. It may be the golden key to fluency. Experts have called it a "compensatory" factor that can make up for a lack of reading skills, especially when the text is particularly difficult. If students are interested, they will keep trying despite the difficulties.

Recent research tells us that fluency improves when students are provided with texts that relate to their interests. If they are interested, they will read more, and the more they read, the more fluent they will become and the more confident they will feel.

You can generate interest in reading in two ways:

- by providing books related to their personal interests
- by providing just plain good books

Linda Gambrell (2015) reminds us that educators "have two equally important reading goals: to teach our students to read and to teach our students to want to read" (p. 259).

Books Related to Students' Interests

Students come to school with already well-developed interests. Even when students are quite young, their interests are strong, stable, and well formed. Ask any six-year-old what they like and … well, they have list. Knowing how to harness those "likes" in reading is key to helping them want to keep reading.

When interviewing students about their perceptions of reading, I always look for that moment when they perk up, lean forward, smile with eyes wide, and tell me what their favorite activities are. Some say, "I love dancing" or "I like to draw," or "Riding my bike," or "I like Super-hero movies," and, occasionally, "Reading. I love to read." I always ask myself how I can leverage my students' existing interests.

All people have likes and predispositions, including adults. That's why some of us naturally gravitate toward the mystery section in a bookstore, while others head for the humor section, and still others end up in the gardening aisle. Some love books about tennis, while others favor books on bridge. Individual interests are unique to each and every reader. I love it when a student tells me about a favorite activity—I know that, soon enough, I will find the perfect book they will want to read.

Teaching Tip: *Want to Know Students' Interests? Ask Them!*

How do we connect students with the books they want to read? One strategy is to hand out reading interest surveys (also called inventories) at the beginning of the school year to find out about your students' reading interests. Then, search for books that match what your students like.

Teacher Jordan says this about using reading interest surveys with his Grade 6 students: "My students love that I recommend books to them based on what they tell me they like. I get help from my school librarian to do this. I couldn't do it without her. The students are usually surprised when I hand them a book on a topic like hockey or music. Or find books set in the outdoors if they tell me they love being outside." To read more about reading interest surveys, see pages 154–155 in Chapter 6.

Just Plain Good Books

Sometimes interest is stimulated not by the student's particular interests but by a particularly good book. It might be a strange topic, a quirky format, melodic language, fabulous illustrations, or just a captivating tale that makes the book interesting.

Have you felt that "gives-me-chills" moment that happens in classrooms when students sit mesmerized as you read aloud from a book? Take *Finding Home: The Journey of Immigrants and Refugees* by Jen Sookfong Lee. This book for middle school explores current issues facing immigrants and refugees by telling first-hand, true, terrifying stories about people who left unsafe living conditions in search of a new life. Books like this open a window to situations and experiences that are far beyond the day-to-day lives of most students we teach.

I recall having my interest caught by Jeff Lemire's book *The Collected Essex County* (2008). It was the first time I had read a graphic novel for an older audience. I was absolutely captivated by the storytelling, the images, and even by my response to it. Before reading this book, I doubted I could ever find a graphic novel as engaging and meaningful as a traditional novel. But the format and the story of Lemire's book just amazed me—I was forever changed as a reader by that book.

I have watched similar transformations take place among students in many primary classrooms with books such as *The Book with No Pictures* by B. J. Novak (a picture book with no pictures) and *The Snowman* by Raymond Briggs (a picture book with no text). Another unique book with no text, *The Mysteries of Harris Burdick* by Chris Van Allsburg, intrigues students in upper elementary and middle school. The sheer novelty of these books entice students as readers.

Today, more than ever, an abundance of exemplary children's and young adult literature offers plenty of options to appeal to every student.

It is encouraging to see more and more books published by and about diverse and racialized people, as well as growing numbers of stories, authors, and illustrators that increase the visibility and positive representations of LGBTQ+ people. Many students see themselves in these texts and want to read them. Further, the inclusion of these books in your classroom encourage acceptance, understanding, and celebration of difference. In a study of readers about books that made a significant difference in their lives, readers said that they

- awakened a new perspective
- modelled identity because readers could see themselves in the book
- provided reassurance and comfort, and confirmed their self-worth and strength
- helped the reader connect with others with the message, "you are not alone"
- gave them the courage to make a change in their lives
- provided acceptance
- helped them understand the world

Teaching Tip

Inherently interesting books have one or more of the following characteristics:

- novel in some way (genre, format, topic, plot, characters, setting)
- surprising
- intense
- strong visual imagery
- easy to comprehend
- personally relevant

Look for books that contain some of these features to share with your students. Ask a librarian, colleague, or a language and literacy professor (such as me) for suggestions. Everyone loves to tell about their favorites.

In my early years of teaching, I did not use students' own interests as an avenue to help them develop as readers. Perhaps because no one had done that for me. As a new Grade 1 teacher, I had done what I thought I was supposed to do: use the basal reading instruction series that the previous teacher had left on the shelf in my new classroom to teach reading. Anyone out there remember Mr. Mugs?

I'm not sure I actually did teach all my students how to read that year. It did help that I understood a bit about the importance of phonics, phonemic awareness, fluency, vocabulary, and comprehension. But, looking back, I realize that I let the program tell me what to do.

Before long, I realized that some children took to the stories in the readers quickly. They benefited from the reading series. Others, however, did not. For the sake of those students, I knew I had to change what I was doing.

Two enthusiastic literacy teachers and authors, Robert McCracken and Marlene McCracken, entered the reading scene in the 1990s. This duo introduced me and many other teachers to new books and texts that were thematically based, predictable, and repetitive—but that also captured the interests of students. The McCrackens are credited with developing a literature-based teaching approach designed to help teachers build children's reading skills and love of reading.

I began sharing books such as Bill Martin, Jr.'s, *Brown, Bear, Brown Bear, What Do You See?* and the wordless picture book, *Rosie's Walk* by Pat Hutchins, which my students loved. They practically jumped up and down at just the moment before I turned the page to see if the fox was going to catch Rosie the Hen on her leisurely walk through the farmyard.

When I made these stories and others based on their structures available to my students, they read them eagerly and fluently. I began to see how I could expand my reading instruction to attract and engage my students' interest. Notice that I said expand, not replace. The components of reading, especially decoding, continued to figure prominently in my Grade 1 program, but now I also accessed rich and appealing literature for practice.

Teaching Tip: *Ways to Promote Interest in Reading*
- Provide independent reading time for students.
- Let students know when you think a particular book or author might interest them because of something you know about them. Ideally, put the book directly into their hands.
- Introduce a variety of books and have the class vote on the one for a read-aloud.
- Invite students' favorite authors into the classroom for virtual visits and question-and-answer sessions.
- Have students find interesting books through a library scavenger hunt.
- Present two books with two different perspectives on a topic. Read and then discuss.

Marilyn, a Grade 4 teacher, tells about her effort to create an open-ended assignment as a way to address the varying fluency needs of the readers in her class.

My class was working on a unit we called, "The Heroes Among Us." We read a number of fiction and non-fiction texts, such as *Kids of Kabul* by Deborah Ellis, *Highway of Heroes* by Kathy Stinson, and *Terry Fox and Me* by Mary Beth Leatherdale.

I suggested to my students that heroes are often very personal. I told them that heroes mean different things to different people. I asked them to choose a hero—it could be someone close to them or it could be someone they admired from afar—and then to find a book to read to inspire them to write about that hero.

The book they chose did not have to be about the person they were writing about. It simply was to be used as inspiration. I kept this assignment purposefully open-ended to make sure the students' reading needs were accommodated. I wanted to see how my students chose a book to read and then connected it to the topic of heroism.

One of my confident readers, Max, chose *The Astonishing Secret of Awesome Man* by Michael Chabon to write about his mom. Max reads on his own in school and at home. Max explained to me that his mom was afraid of spiders, but she pretends not to be. That reminded him of Awesome Man, who appears very brave and unafraid throughout the entire book and then, at the end, comes home to his mom.

Another student, Mary Beth, decided quickly she wanted to write about her dad. She was not confident, however, that she could find a book that reminded her of him and that she would also want to read. I was worried that if she chose a book that was too difficult to read fluently, she would lose interest. Fluency predicts interest, after all. Mary Beth did not have the reading repertoire that Max had. She needed more support to build her confidence.

I asked Mary Beth what she liked to do with her dad, and she said, "Go on walks." Knowing this, I nudged Mary Beth toward the book *Owl Moon* by Jane Yolen, a book I knew that she would be able to read independently and might inspire her to write about her dad. I watched as Mary Beth took the book to her desk, read the story, and looked at the illustrations intently.

Two students with different levels of fluency and confidence as readers. This meant they had different needs as readers and, therefore, two different reactions to this activity. Knowing this was key to finding the right text for Mary Beth to use with this reading and writing task.

Using Interest to Promote Fluency

Students who are interested in reading about a topic ...

... focus their attention on what they read.

... persist in the reading task.

... understand what they read.

Students who are not interested in reading about a topic …
>   … appear bored, indifferent, or detached.
>   … do not understand what they read.
>   … choose to quit reading.

You can take three steps to help interest feed fluency and fluency feed interest:
1. Take time to gain insight into students' interests.
2. Seek books and other reading materials that meet students' interests.
3. Find opportunities to broaden students' interests by providing books that are not related to their interests but are just amazingly good books.

Collaborative Reading Opportunities

The interactions between the student and his or her teacher and class are important to developing intrinsic motivation. Collaboration during the reading process can prevent students from feeling lost as they read and create a sense of shared purpose around reading.
—Natalie Saaris (2016)

Research has shown that subjecting individual students to practicing reading aloud in front of the entire class adds a great deal of anxiety to the process. Instead of reading practice, it feels more like performance practice.

But there is a way for the whole class to practice reading together: collaborative reading practice. By reading aloud together, as a class, in pairs, or in groups, students work within what Lev Vygotsky calls their zone of proximal development (ZPD) (Vygotsky, 1978). In an article on using choral reading to improve reading fluency, Harriet Bessette (2020) reminds us that "the difference between what students can do without help and what they can do with help is brought to the fore during either peer-assisted or teacher-led choral reading." The benefits of collaborative reading experiences are numerous and include the following:

- More-fluent readers support less-fluent readers.
- Students benefit from equal participation.
- Positive interdependence develops.
- Students' enthusiasm for reading spreads.

Have you tried using collaborative reading in your classroom yet? It's worth a try. Some groups of students respond with vigor. But always let your students' responses to this approach guide you. If some students appear less motivated to read aloud with others, be sure you give them the opportunity to read in another way.

One of my favorite choral reading examples was documented in the film, *The Secret of Will: One Grade 2 Class + William Shakespeare = A Journey of a Lifetime.* In this film, a group of adolescent students reflects about choral reading Shakespeare plays rewritten for Grade 2 by their amazing teacher, Lois Burdett. Burdett created an amazing Shakespeare Can Be Fun! series of plays for young children, complete with rhyming language. Yes, you read that correctly: for young children! These rewritten plays were accompanied by her students' own drawings and writing.

It is wild to see six- and seven-year-olds from an elementary school in Stratford, Ontario, embrace learning and reading about William Shakespeare and his plays. The students read and read and read, becoming increasingly fluent over the course of the year. And much of that reading was choral reading. One student summed up the reading experience perfectly, "It always seemed like we were all in it together."

Key Strategies to Help You Teach Fluency

In the following pages of this chapter, I have gathered both new and familiar instructional strategies and practices from teachers, researchers, and my own experience. You can use them to develop students' fluency skills while building their motivation for reading. These nine strategies highlight fluency but also build capacity in the other components of reading—decoding, vocabulary, and comprehension. They are

1. Get students reading to one another in groups
2. Get students reading together in pairs
3. Stage a choral reading
4. Stage a poetry academy
5. Stage readers theatre
6. Try tongue twisters
7. Make time for independent reading
8. Keep tabs on where your students are at
9. Practice retelling with a story vine

1. Get Students Reading to One Another in Groups

Assisted reading-fluency strategies build confidence and nudge students toward independence. "Assisted" refers to the support students get from reading aloud with other people: with other students, with the teacher, with a more-experienced reading buddy from another grade, or with an audiotape. Reading aloud with others is a great way to help students develop their fluency skills. By having students read aloud in pairs or groups, you can make this strategy about reading practice rather than performance practice.

The student-led read-aloud gives students a collaborative reading experience that supports them individually and collectively in the classroom. Regie Routman (2005) tells us that "students learn more when they are able to talk to one another and be actively involved" (p. 207). For many of us, reading is a solitary act. At the same time, learning to read and maintaining a love of reading are both supported by a socially interactive reading community.

Collaboration and talk matter to adult readers, too. It is one of the reasons that people join book clubs. I love being part of a book club so I can find out about new books to read and discuss what we have read. Also important—for me and

I suspect others—is that book clubs offer opportunities to get together socially, talk together, and share the reading experience.

Even for something as seemingly simple as reading aloud, encourage students to practice beforehand. The student-led read-aloud works best with small groups of students so that fluency and comprehension—and not performance—take centre stage in reading. Try this strategy with a variety of texts, student groupings, and subjects. After a few run-throughs using this strategy, ask your students what they think of it.

Teaching Tip: *Pull Back the Curtain*

Let your students know what you do to prepare for a read-aloud. Perhaps you read the book or the text excerpt once, twice, even three times to make sure it sounds right before reading it aloud to them. It is good for your students to know that you might stumble on words the first time you read a book aloud. Pull away the curtain and show them that reading aloud takes time and preparation. The message might sink in a little more if you show students a video of you reading a book the first time so they can see the difference between your cold reading and your polished reading.

STEP BY STEP:

Peer Up and Prepare (PUP) Read-Alouds

How to begin. Choose a novel chapter, a short story, a textbook chapter, or anything else that you want students to read and understand. Take the time to read the chosen text beforehand to decide if it is one that students will be able to read and understand.

Create peer groups. Preplan student groups of four to five readers. (Always use your discretion to group students in larger or smaller groups.) Aim for groups with a diversity of reading skills. For this activity, readers support one another to read fluently and understand the text.

Section the text. Divide the text into sections and look for natural breaks where it would be appropriate to switch from one reader to another.

Plan reading sections. Beforehand, link individual students to sections of the text thoughtfully, making use of what you know about your readers. More proficient readers could read longer sections of text, while less proficient readers could read crucial shorter pieces of information. For longer texts, avoid assigning exceptionally long sections, and instead assign each reader two or more shorter sections. Make sure that graphs, photographs, figures, and other information are assigned to readers as part of the text. You want to help students see how reading everything on a page contributes to their understanding.

Prepare vocabulary. Make a list of vocabulary in the text that could pose difficulties for fluency and comprehension. Mark or note where these words appear in the text.

Get things started. Assign students to their groups. Provide the vocabulary list to each group, along with a thesaurus and a pronunciation guide. Review all the vocabulary as a class. Doing this beforehand helps students navigate the most challenging pronunciation and comprehension hurdles they will face.

Introduce the text. Introduce the text to students, giving them as much context as necessary to comprehend the reading. You may do this in several ways. Some examples of ways to introduce a new text are provided in Inventive Ways to Introduce a New Book on pages 76–77.

Teaching Tip

Help students see how reading everything on a page contributes to their understanding.

Students practice individually. Provide students with the text and the sections they will be reading. Give them adequate practice time to read their own sections silently. Make allowances for students who need to sub-vocalize while practicing by spacing students out and letting them move to comfortable places in the classroom or library if it is available. During this time, students can ask you and their group members for any help needed during practice time.

Make tracking visible. Some students need and appreciate a way to track the text to help them read fluently. Provide colorful pieces of paper, shaped like a thick bookmark, that students can put on the page under each sentence or paragraph as they read it. (Avoid white paper on white, as this can interfere with effective tracking.)

Students read aloud in their peer groups. Next, you might say, "Now that you have practiced reading your parts of the text, it is time to put it all together and read aloud together in your groups." Students take turns by reading aloud their assigned, practiced sections. In this way, reading is interactive and collaborative.

Monitor and reflect. Observe students by visiting the groups one at a time. The classroom will be noisy and energetic with engaged, active readers. This is a good time to take informal anecdotal records of your observations related to fluency and other reading skills as students read. At the end of the session, use some after-reading strategies to help students focus on their comprehension of the text. You might consider asking students for feedback by asking them to complete exit slips with a question or two about this reading strategy.

· ·

In Julie Ann's Classroom: A Pronunciation Lesson in Middle School

Sometimes difficulty in pronunciation can slow down fluency. Grade 8 teacher Julie Ann watches for signs of such difficulties. She moves from group to group as her students read novels in book clubs. I watch a group of four students finish reading a chapter from the book *Peak* by Roland Smith. They talk about what they have read and understood from the story so far. Then they each share vocabulary from the chapter that they want to work on. One student records the words as the others find them in the text. After all group members have had a chance to suggest words, they compare their list with the one that their teacher has provided as a guide. The two lists are almost identical.

The first word the students focus on is *photographer*. One student says, "I know how to say *photo* and *photograph*, but I always mess up saying *photographer*." He pronounces the word with emphasis on the first syllable just as he would when pronouncing *photograph*. "See?" he says. The students laugh together. Another student agrees, "Me too."

Julie Ann listens in and asks the students to write out the three words: *photo*, *photograph*, and *photographer*. She asks, "What do each of these words mean?" No problem. They know what the words mean.

She then asks, "What is tricky about the words?" The students explain that the third word is hard to say. She agrees and tells them it is because the second syllable needs to be stressed instead of the first, and that when they do that, it changes the vowel sound.

Julie Ann then asks the students to clap the syllables as they say each part of the word. She tells them they are going to stress the second syllable and they will also change its vowel sound from a long vowel *o* sound (as it sounds in *photo*) to a short vowel *o* sound (as in *hot*). The students change the vowel sound and put the emphasis on the second clap. They do this several times, making the second clap louder and changing the syllable sound, until they all pronounce the word correctly.

Julie Ann reviews a decoding strategy she has just taught: "When you come to a word that is causing you trouble, because you aren't sure how to pronounce it, you can do what I do and use a pronunciation app." She takes out her phone and shows them a pronunciation app that they can use anytime they are unsure how to pronounce a word. "And when you do that," she added, "you have a new word that is part of your vocabulary."

Julie Ann is correct. Students need opportunities to say and hear new words, spell them, read them fluently in context, and learn what they mean to truly make them their own.

2. Get Students Reading Together in Pairs

Partner reading takes a solitary activity and makes it a social one.

Students love to work together when they read. They love to work together, period. They may be unaware of how fluency develops when reading together, but you aren't. Partner reading takes a solitary activity and makes it a social one. In pairs, the reading stakes are low, which makes it great for practicing fluency. There is no performance aspect to reading with a partner. Because of that, this strategy can be used with students without having them practice reading before they get together.

. . . .

STEP BY STEP:

"Pair and Prepare" Read-Alouds

How to begin. To prepare, read the text beforehand to ensure that it is a text that students will be able to read and understand. This first step is sometimes missed, but it is crucial to ensure that the text is one that students can read on their own.

Pair students. Students with different reading fluency levels often work well together as pairs because the better reader can occasionally help the other reader along. If two students who struggle with reading are asked to read together (without your oversight), they may struggle, lose confidence, and find something else to do. While you will often make the decisions about which students to put together, it is sometimes helpful to use the find-a-friend method, too, for paired reading. (Over time, you will want to vary how you pair students, so that they get to enjoy the method they prefer from time to time.)

Prepare student for the reading. This step is a must and can be accomplished in several ways. Overall, though, you want to ensure that the readers have sufficient background information and context to read the text fluently and with comprehension. Your overview can be done with the whole class prior to partner reading.

Inventive Ways to Introduce a New Book

- Survey the text with students, looking at the cover, title, pictures, and diagrams, and read the first paragraph aloud.
- Ask students to predict what a story or non-fiction text will be about, based on the title, cover, or even a flip through to see illustrations.
- Create or review a character, setting, or plot map with the students.
- View a short video that sets the context and background knowledge needed for the reading.

- Have students complete the first two columns of a K-W-L-H chart about the topic of the book (K: What I already know about this topic; W: What I want to learn by reading this text; L: What I have learned while reading this text; and H: How I will learn more after reading this text. (Ogle, 1986).)
- Activate students' prior knowledge about the text's topic, for example, through a picture walk: show students the pictures in a book before reading the text. This gives readers the chance to consider what the story is about. For older students, use an anticipation guide: a set of statements that relate to the text. Students agree or disagree with the statements, and then check them during the reading.
- Make a list of vocabulary that students might find challenging in the text, review the words and phrases with students using the whiteboard or chart paper, and show students where in the text these words appear.

Read together. The pairs of students now read the text together. They decide to either choral read or use a "my turn, your turn" approach to reading sections of the text aloud. You might suggest choral reading for students who need practice with fluency.

Monitor and reflect. Visit each pair of students while they read. Write informal anecdotal records of observations about students' fluency and other reading skills. Lastly, employ after-reading strategies that help students focus on their comprehension of the text.

· ·

In Joy's Classroom: Using Partner Reading to Create Bonds

Joy shared with me how she uses peer groups in her Grade 2/3 classroom.

I use peer groups to help my students develop friendships, find out what they have in common, read together, and learn from one another. Because I have two age groups represented in my classroom, I want to help students think about each other, not as Grade 2s and Grade 3s but as members of our class community.

This past year, I had two students, one in Grade 2 and one in Grade 3, whose reading proficiency levels were similar (one was slightly more fluent than the other). They were both really interested in our rocks and minerals unit, but they had not yet connected with each other even after two months of school. I felt this was because of their different ages.

When students were deciding on projects to research for Fridays' genius hour, I suggested to these two girls that they might want to work together on a topic. I told them I knew they shared an interest in a particular topic—their eyes lit up and they looked at me and one another and smiled—it was a shared interest in rocks and minerals. Even though their reading fluency was not at quite the same level, they become fast reading friends.

3. Stage a Choral Reading

Do you remember choral reading in grade school? Perhaps your class learned a poem to recite at a choral reading festival? Choral readings figured prominently in my own early education. I can recite most of Dennis Lee's poem "Alligator Pie" to this day, as a result.

Choral reading is a simple strategy: students read a text aloud in unison. It does not have to be memorized or a performance.

My most recent memory of choral reading was observing a lesson in which Ryan, a Grade 5 teacher, shared with his students the poem "If I Were In Charge of the World" by Judith Viorst. Ryan began by reading the poem aloud to his students. Then he and his students read the poem aloud all together once, twice, three times. By the third reading, Ryan could no longer be heard. And the reading flowed. The students were enthusiastic, raising their voices, using phrasing effectively, emphasizing words like *I* and *world*. No one appeared nervous. Everyone participated. It was what I might call low-stakes reading. One teacher said this about choral reading, "When you read all together with the children first, everybody experiences success at the same time."

Students are not even aware that they are practicing their reading fluency while having fun in a choral reading. The great thing is that everybody must read but no one is singled out for embarrassment. This technique is most often used with young children, but I think that limitation is a bit of a mistake. As students get older, they might still need the safety in numbers that reading chorally provides.

Why use choral reading in the classroom?
- works with large or small groups
- works with or without you reading along
- works for a variety of subjects
- good for fiction and non-fiction texts alike
- brings together more- and less-fluent readers
- provides extra practice
- is enjoyed even by older students!

· ·

STEP BY STEP: ## Choral Reading

How to begin. Choose a text that students will read all together. All the following texts lend themselves to choral reading:

- morning messages
- poems
- nursery rhymes
- picture books with repeated patterns, stanzas, or prediction
- choral reading scripts
- songs
- sonnets
- soliloquies and stanzas from plays
- spoken word poetry
- speeches

Here are a few popular texts I have seen used effectively in elementary and middle school classrooms, but there are so many. Always choose texts that interest your students.

- *You Read to Me, I'll Read to You* by Mary Ann Hoberman and Michael Emberley (primary grades)
- *The Word Collector* by Peter H. Reynolds (intermediate grades)
- *I am Phoenix: Poems for Two Voices* by Paul Fleischman (middle school)
- *The Hill We Climb and Other Poems* by Amanda Gorman (high school)

Visibility. Students need to be able to see the text for choral reading whether you project it onto a screen, show it on a piece of chart paper, share it through a video, or provide each student with a copy of the text.

Teacher models reading. Read the text aloud first, tracking words and lines. Model reading the text fluently:

- Read in a normal, relaxed tone of voice.

- Read clearly and slowly.
- Pause where punctuation requires it.
- Emphasize the rhythms and sounds of specific words in the text.

Prepare vocabulary. Make a list of vocabulary that students might find challenging in the text. Include words that are hard to pronounce, as well as words that may be unfamiliar. You might review these words with students using the whiteboard or chart paper, and then show them where in the text these words appear. It is helpful to write these words out phonetically for students to see.

All together. Have everyone read the text aloud together two to three times to become familiar with the text, vocabulary, pronunciation, phrasing, and expression. All students read every line of the text in unison. Everyone participates and no one is singled out.

Extensions. The choral reading can end there. Or it can be extended in a variety of ways. Here are three extension possibilities:

- *Concurrent choral reading*: Divide the class into small groups of students who then continue to choral read the text as a group, adding in movement or gestures if they wish. They can put their own spin on the reading and then share it with the whole class.
- *Back-and-forth choral reading*: Divide students into two groups. One group reads a section, and then the other continues. The reading continues in a back-and-forth manner from beginning to end.
- *Echo choral reading*: You or a group of students read one line or section of the text, and the others echo it back, matching the speed, expression, and phrasing. Students might be asked to mimic the way the first group reads a section, for instance, in a whisper, accompanied by hand clapping, or with a particular emotion.

4. Stage a Poetry Academy

The reading fluency strategy called the "poetry academy" (Wilfong, 2008) is like choral reading but with a few notable differences. It has a performance aspect to it—they perform for each other in small groups or pairs—but students work together and have as much time as they need to prepare, so it should not be a stressful exercise. If you've never used poetry in the classroom, don't be shy. Just be frank with your students and let them know that you are trying something new and want to see how they do with it.

Bring books of poetry into the classroom related to a wide variety of themes and disciplines, such as sports, music, drama, science, math, social studies, social justice, and art. That way, there is something for everyone. Students work together in small groups or pairs to choose a few of the poetry books together. If they are like students I have worked with, they will be excited to find poems about topics that interest them, such as *The Crossover* by Kwame Alexander about basketball, *Feel the Beat* by Marilyn Singer about dance music, and *Science Verse* by Jon Scieszka about, you guessed it, science.

In every small group or pair, each student selects a poem he or she can read independently. They then practice reading their chosen poems aloud in unison, helping each other prepare, until it is performance ready. They then present their poems to each other, often in very humorous and engaging ways.

Teaching Tip

Some teachers opt to have their students choose popular song lyrics (approved by the teacher) to use for the poetry academy. Teachers tell me that the buy-in at the middle school level is sometimes much greater for song lyrics than it is for poetry. You know your students best, and so can best judge if this is a good option for your class.

5. Stage Readers Theatre

Readers theatre performances can be informal or formal, simple or polished. But they are always a team effort!

Readers theatre is a motivational strategy drawn from the dramatic arts, whereby students read scripts aloud to improve their reading fluency. Like the poetry academy, it combines practice and performance. Students have the chance to practice reading their scripts expressively and fluently, and then they share their reading with an audience. You can help students as they practice reading a script or text multiple times before performing it for small or large groups of peers.

Performances can be informal or formal, simple or polished. But they are always a team effort! The key to success is your thoughtful consideration of each students' level of readiness. Chat with each student about their comfort and stress levels before deciding on their readiness for performance.

While many published scripts are available for readers theatre, your students might enjoy creating their own scripts based on any other texts they are reading. And they might find it easier. After all, we can all read what we write.

In Trevor's Classroom: Song Lyrics for Readers Theatre

Trevor uses the readers theatre strategy in his Grade 8 class on Mondays and Fridays. This enthusiastic math teacher was given the opportunity to teach a reading option in middle school. He told me that he used picture books when he first introduced readers theatre to his students, but he found that his middle school students were less than enthusiastic to use these books "for kids" to perform in front of their peers.

Trevor asked his students what texts they would like to use. They told him they wanted to use song lyrics, naturally. So Trevor did a pivot. That's what it means to keep your students' interests in mind in any reading approach. Trevor created a set of guidelines he uses with his students for readers theatre that I will describe for you here.

Beforehand, Trevor talks to his students about the strategy of readers theatre, telling them about its purpose to increase fluency, improve comprehension, and involve everyone in reading in a non-threatening way. He shares the kinds of texts that students might use, guidelines for preparation, and the criteria for grading.

Trevor explains that over the coming months, every student will have the opportunity to select a song for readers theatre. Each song-selector will work with their group of five or six students over the course of a week to create a performance. (The groups remain constant over five or six weeks—long enough that every student gets to be song-selector once.)

On Mondays, student groups meet together and discuss their ideas. The song selector lets Trevor know which song lyrics the group would like to use. Trevor checks all the lyrics to make sure they are appropriate for school. He makes copies of each chosen text (usually over the noon-hour) so that all students have their own copy on which to highlight text and make notes. Students have time during this first session to decide how they would like to parse the text, to make decisions about who will read which parts, and to decide when they might come together to practice. Students also discuss the vocabulary, phrasing, and pronunciation of the lyrics. Trevor visits each group, answering questions and assisting with pronunciation and aspects of the performance.

During the week, students are encouraged to work in their readers theatre groups at the beginning or ending of class, when other work is finished, or when they have free time. Trevor says that the students often use some of their noon-hour and breaks during the day to work together. He provides them with a checklist to keep them on track.

Checklist for Readers Theatre

Students in Your Group: _____

1.	Has your group chosen a text?	Yes	No
2.	Has your teacher approved the text?	Yes	No
3.	Has your group discussed and chosen roles?	Yes	No
4.	Have members of your group highlighted each of your parts?	Yes	No
5.	Has the group practiced the reading at least three times?		

1st time____   2nd time____   3rd time____

Questions to ask the teacher:

Pembroke Publishers ©2021 *Sometimes Reading Is Hard* by Robin Bright ISBN 978-1-55138-351-4

On Fridays, the groups perform their song lyric texts for the rest of the class during readers theatre. Trevor says that some groups bring in props and make-up, while others simply do their reading. These decisions are up to the students. In some instances, Trevor gives students the opportunity to film their performances and play the recording for their peers. This helps with feelings of nervousness about performing in front of others and lets the student performers have a chance to view their own presentations.

Rubric for Readers Theatre Performances

Students in Your Group: _____

Areas for Growth	Criteria	Exceeded Expectations
	Students read the lyrics with confidence and expression.	
	The performance included gestures, eye contact, and props to support the performance.	
	Students worked well together and shared responsibilities to prepare for the performance.	

Pembroke Publishers ©2021 *Sometimes Reading Is Hard* by Robin Bright ISBN 978-1-55138-351-4

Extensions. You can extend this technique by involving the whole class in choral reading. Trevor offers this suggestion:

> Once a week, I print off the lyrics for the current top-40 songs for my class. Students vote on the song they would like to read that week. I find the chosen song on YouTube (lyrics only, not the official video) and play the song with the lyrics showing up on the screen. The students follow along by reading the lyrics on hard copies. After we listen to the song once or twice, we read the song as a class. Then, I assign various parts of the song to students, usually in pairs, and we read the song again with each student reading aloud one or two lines of the song. My students love this activity and I feel it was one of my most successful strategies in helping students read more fluently.

The goal of readers theatre is to give students reading practice with the components of reading, especially fluency, in a supportive and socially interactive classroom community. The wonderful thing is that students themselves can suggest texts. Each time they choose the text themselves, you can rest assured that your students are engaged, and, most important, they will read!

6. Try Tongue Twisters

Fishing for a little fun in your focus on fluency? Add tongue twisters to the mix! They provide an entertaining, light-hearted way for students to practice pronunciation and fluency (both oral fluency and reading fluency). Tongue twisters encourage students to chew over words, not just for their spellings or meanings but for their sounds.

When reading specialist Sheila Stern introduced "Fun Fridays with a Focus on Fluency" to her students in Grades 3, 4, and 5, she found students' fluency made huge improvements. And her students loved it. Tongue twisters can be used at any grade level and can be tailored to specific reading needs as well. You can find tongue twisters that zero in on specific letter sounds, patterns, consonant blends, and vowel sounds. The great thing is that students aren't intimidated by tongue twisters because, let's face it, they are hard for you, too.

STEP BY STEP: Teaching Tongue Twisters

Start small. I love to start a class on tongue twisters, whether for school-aged students or pre-service teachers, with one word: *toyboat*. I write this word on the board, and everyone reads it aloud. Not too difficult yet. Then I suggest they try and repeat it three times, then four and even five times. Of course, it gets progressively more difficult because each syllable requires the mouth to take a completely different shape. Try it! The difficulty of saying the word over and over again successfully, according to experts, has to do with the placement of the tongue and how the brain processes sounds. For such a simple word, this is quite a complicated process.

Shorties. Next, find or make a variety of tongue twisters for students to read. These can incorporate sounds for decoding practice as well as vocabulary students are encountering in their reading. Write these out on cards and give them to pairs of students to practice reading together. Remember, collaboration works wonders to help fluency along. I have seen teachers laminate these cards and keep them in a box or link them with a binder ring for ease of use.

Tongue twisters can be alliterative, especially if you want your students to see the relationship between certain sounds and letters, but they don't need to be. You can use them to provide fluency practice for a variety of sounds in language and vocabulary. Here are a few for you to try:

- "Five frivolous friends followed Frankenstein."
- "Ethan eats elegant Easter eggs."
- "Yellow butter, purple jelly, red jam, black bread."
- "Any noise annoys an oyster, but a noisy noise annoys an oyster more."

Twister books. Find a set of books with tongue twisters that are just right for your students' grade level and interests. Here are a few to get you started:

- *A Greyhound, a Groundhog* by Emily Jenkins (ages 5–7)
- *Tongue Twisters for Kids* by Riley Weber (ages 6–10)
- *Orangutang Tongs: Poems to Tangle Your Tongue* by Jon Agee (ages 4–8)
- *Double Trouble in Walla Walla* by Andrew Clements (ages 7–11)

Watching the results. If students have access to tablets, phones, or other technology with video capability, encourage them to capture themselves reading their tongue twisters to view or share with others. If you teach young children, have them look in a mirror as they say the tongue-twister words. This lets them see how they move their mouths to make certain sounds. This adds a metacognitive aspect to the "game."

Reflection. While some tongue twisters are easily memorized, encourage your students to read the twisters as they repeat them. This will emphasize fluency. After working with tongue twisters for several weeks, ask your students if they think it has helped with their reading fluency. This is an important step, especially with older readers who can and should be encouraged to reflect on their own reading progress throughout the school year.

Teaching Tip

Any time students are practicing reading aloud, encourage them to self-assess using a checklist like the one below.

Self-Assessment for Reading Aloud

My goal is to _____

	1 Not Often	2 Often	3 Always
1. Read all phrases as a unit.	☺	☺☺	☺☺☺
2. Pause at punctuation.	☺	☺☺	☺☺☺
3. Use expression that works with the meaning.	☺	☺☺	☺☺☺
4. Read at a rate that sounds like speech.	☺	☺☺	☺☺☺
5. Read accurately with only one or two errors.	☺	☺☺	☺☺☺
6. Self-correct errors.	☺	☺☺	☺☺☺

Pembroke Publishers ©2021 *Sometimes Reading Is Hard* by Robin Bright ISBN 978-1-55138-351-4

7. Make Time for Independent Reading

Practice, practice, and more practice will help students develop the fluency they need to read successfully. If you want to improve as a skier, a driver, a dancer, a singer—or anything else, really—it takes practice. Timothy Shanahan points out that "the best readers are the ones that read the most." It seems obvious, but it bears repeating. Make sure students have dedicated time during the school day—every day—to read.

Educators such as Cris Tovani, Larry Swartz, Shelley Stagg Peterson, and Donalyn Miller have championed the independent reading movement of the past few years and all I can say is, thank goodness!

Donalyn Miller famously tells her upper elementary students at the beginning of the school year that each of them will read 40 books over the course of the year. Forty books! Notably, she doesn't set this out as a challenge, which would

Teaching Tip

Perhaps you recall the number of hours that Malcolm Gladwell says (in his book *Outliers*) are needed "to bring greatness to a skill." I am not sure I agree with his number of 10 000 hours, but I do agree that "practice makes you better than you were yesterday, most of the time" (Macnamara, 2019). So ask yourself: how are you helping your students put in the hours needed to become skilled, fluent, passionate readers?

84   *Sometimes Reading Is Hard*

likely lead some students to disengage. Instead, she sets it out as a promise. Miller is quick to point out that even if her students don't meet that goal, they will still have read more books than they did the previous year. She focuses on helping students reach their potential as readers through self-selected reading. Miller writes,

> Ten books or twenty books are not enough to instill a love of reading in students. They must choose and read many books for themselves in order to catch the reading bug. By setting the requirement as high as I do, I ensure that students must have a book going constantly. Without the need to read a book every single day to stay on top of my requirement, students would read as little as they could. They might not internalize independent reading habits if my requirement expected less from them.

Independent reading is one strategy among many that you can use to address the components of reading. I strongly endorse it for helping your students learn to read fluently and inspiring them to want to read. The goal of this strategy is to create an authentic opportunity for students to develop fluency and to see themselves as competent and engaged readers.

Fifteen Minutes Is Magic!

Recognizing the importance of providing time and space in classrooms for students to read books they choose for themselves is the first step. Carving out 15 minutes a day can make all the difference. That length of time is considered consequential in helping students improve their decoding, fluency, vocabulary, and comprehension reading skills. And it's so easy to make this a part of your daily routine.

Depending on the age of the students, you might start with five minutes of independent reading time and then move to a ten- to fifteen-minute block of time. Slowly increase this time as your timetable permits and as students become familiar and comfortable with managing themselves during this independent time.

Teacher and author of *Passionate Readers*, Pernille Ripp, says that, when she taught elementary school, she had the flexibility to give students 30 minutes a day to read independently. Now, as a middle school teacher, she devotes the first ten to fifteen minutes of a one-hour period to reading—always!

Teaching Tip: *Give Students Ownership of Reading Time*

There are many different names and acronyms that refer to independent reading in school such as DEAR Time (Drop Everything and Read), OTTER (Our Time to Enjoy Reading), and SURF (Silent Uninterrupted Reading Fun). As you learn more about how to organize and manage independent reading, share these names and acronyms with your students. Ask them for other suggestions, too, and then vote on the class favorite. This helps students to take ownership of independent reading as a valuable aspect of their school day.

[C]hildren should be given the opportunity to enjoy reading and take ownership of their own learning. These goals can be accomplished by offering students a limited variety of reading options and by providing time to read independently.
—Researcher Julie Fraumeni-McBride, 2017

Teaching Tip

Carving out 15 minutes a day can make all the difference. And it's so easy to make this a part of your daily routine!

Guided Choice Really Matters

During reading time, you will see students busily reading chapter books, picture books, graphic novels, comics, magazines, and informational books. But time to read should not be a free-for-all. You should never completely fade into the background. Nothing replaces an involved, knowledgeable, and responsive teacher. Experts agree that it is up to the teacher to make reading time worthwhile. This means that you can and should make suggestions based on what you know about your students as readers.

We know from the previous chapter that one way to guide students is to help them find just-right texts. You may recall that these are books that meet students' needs as readers. You can also encourage them to seek books that they find personally interesting—books they would *love* to read. If they have never found a book that they genuinely loved, they might not believe this is possible. That's where guided choice makes the difference.

I recall taking my Grade 4 students to the school library for their weekly visits. Even after 20 minutes or more of perusing the shelves, interacting with the book displays, sharing favorite titles with their friends, and pulling books to look at, I often heard a few students say, "I can't find anything to read."

I would talk with these students and get a sense of their likes. Together we would ask the librarian for some suggestions. To make sure the books were ones that the students could read independently, we looked through them together and the students tried out reading a few sentences. If they struggled too much— and they often knew it themselves—they put the book back and we continued looking. Eventually, everyone left with a couple of books they wanted to read and could read. That's guided choice.

8. Keep Tabs on Where Your Students Are At

At this point, it is understandable to wonder how you will keep track of students' reading progress, especially their fluency, during independent reading. Once the routines for reading independently are in place and students get better at choosing just-right books for themselves, you can use your time with students to observe, confer, record, and set a goal.

Several formative assessment tools are at your disposal for keeping track of how your students are progressing not only in fluency but with other reading skills as well. These tools are for daily use and complement the screening and diagnostic reading assessments discussed in Chapter 2. Remember that screening and diagnostic testing measure students' strengths and needs in all components of reading. They are best used at the beginning and end of the school year, while formative assessments help keep you apprised of students' progress *during* the year.

Formative assessment tools are less formal than the screening and diagnostic tests and range from status-of-the-class charts to running records, reading conferences, anecdotal comments, and self-reports. I will describe a few of these tools in the next section and let you know how they can help you keep track of students' progress as fluent readers.

Status-of-the-Class Charts

You may be familiar with Nancie Atwell's well-known status-of-the-class routine from her seminal book *In the Middle*. She designed this effective accountability system to get ongoing information from students quickly and efficiently about their reading process. Did you know these are helpful in gauging students' reading fluency?

Prepare. First create a chart with column headings for your students' names, the titles of the books they are reading, the page number they are on, and the date. (See below for an example.) Teachers tell me that Google sheets work well for this purpose.

Check in. Once a week or more, call on students at the beginning of their independent reading session and ask for the information you need to fill out the status-of-the-class chart. The routine takes only about 90 seconds but gives you important information to look at in determining how best to support student reading at that moment.

Analyze it. The status-of-the-class chart can help you pinpoint information:

- what book each student is reading
- how long it takes a student to read a text
- when a student seems stuck and not moving forward with a text
- when a student cannot seem to find a book that they want to or can finish
- when a student is on fire, reading books they enjoy
- what students' reading interests are (and what they are not)
- when to suggest new books to students
- when students need a reading conference with you

Status of the Class

Week of _____

Student	Book Title	Current Page; N=New; Q=Quit; F=Finished				
		M	**T**	**W**	**Th**	**F**
Keegan	The One & Only Ivan	37				

Pembroke Publishers ©2021 *Sometimes Reading Is Hard* by Robin Bright ISBN 978-1-55138-351-4

Refer to it. This ongoing compilation of data can provide a window into your students' levels of reading fluency because you can see how long it takes a student to complete a chapter or a section of the book they are reading, and how fluency improves through the school year. Since fluency is a growth process, it is helpful to monitor it over time. Your data will show when students are developing into fluent readers and when they are struggling. Bring it to teacher-parent meetings, so you can provide parents with facts. It can also be useful as a starting point for discussion in longer reading conferences with students.

Reading Conferences

Experience and common sense tell us that ongoing guidance can aid students who are reading on their own. With that in mind, plan to meet with individual students for short but meaningful reading conferences. These meetings should not overshadow the reading time, but they should add to the reading experience. Students should come away from a conference with a deeper understanding of some aspect of their reading, like fluency, for instance. You should come away with greater insight into your students' reading strengths and challenges.

Try to begin reading conferences the very first week of school. Use them to get to know students as readers as quickly as possible. Have students read aloud to you for a few minutes, informally monitoring word accuracy, pacing, phrasing, and expression. This will help you to distinguish between students who are likely fluent readers and those who are not. Don't forget to ask one or two questions so students can show you their comprehension of what they read. Hold two to three conferences a day till you have seen all your students, heard each of them read, and have a baseline understanding of who your students are as readers.

You can use the reading conference to take a short running record, provide individualized instruction, discuss the students' reactions and connections to a text, affirm students' choices, or simply demonstrate the importance of reading. You can gather information that will inform your teaching. For example, reading conferences can help you know when to pivot your teaching toward specific reading skills (such as decoding, sight words, or pronunciation).

Here are a few tips to keep in mind for conferences during daily reading time:

- Make conversations brief but meaningful.
- Keep conversations positive.
- Share your own reading experiences and insights.
- Ask students about their reading choices and monitor where necessary.
- Listen to students read.
- Provide encouragement and suggestions for further reading.
- Take notes for future instructional possibilities. (It is impossible to remember everything that is said during a reading conference.)

Teaching Tip

Use what you know about your students to offer specific books to individuals. I promise you that anything you recommend will build buzz. Former International Literacy President Linda Gambrell says, "Kids read what we bless." The more you read, the better you are able to help students find texts that they are interested in.

Teaching Tip: *Help Students Notice the Structures of Text*

The reading conference is the perfect time to improve students' fluency by helping them notice the structure of the books they are reading individually. Students in elementary and middle school love the National Geographic Readers series for children in Kindergarten to Grade 5. A favorite is *Cats vs. Dogs* by Elizabeth Carney. This book provides an exemplar for the compare-and-contrast structure. In a reading conference, find out what students noticed about this structure and then show them the illustrated glossary. Top-ten "cool" facts are also included. Students' reading fluency improves when students notice the structures of texts. They anticipate what is coming next in a text, which serves to enhance the speed, accuracy, and expression of their reading. (For more on text structures, see Chapter 5.)

In Marco's Classroom: Extend the Reading Conference through Reading Tell-Alls

Middle school teacher Marco gives his students the opportunity to make a short video he calls a reading tell-all. It's a way to get students talking frankly about their reading experiences, which engages students with reading and also provides Marco with invaluable information.

In a reading tell-all, students share their reading perceptions using a media app such as Padlet or Zigazoo. Students respond to prompts by making brief videos in which they talk about their reading experience. These videos are shared on a digital notice board or wall that can be made private to be viewed by the teacher alone. Students from pre-school to high school can use these free apps. Marco sets up a reading tell-all corner area in the classroom for one week, three times a year.

Marco told me a little more about his experience using the reading tell-all:

I love the reading tell-alls! Maybe because of the name, "tell-all," which most of my students are all pretty familiar with through TV shows. The tell-alls they are familiar with usually contain some kind of honest, tell-it-like-it-is talk. They understand that the purpose is to share something that I might not know or that they haven't shared before.

I have had students say things like, "When you started reading the book *Wonder* [to the class], I thought it was going to be kind of lame, but now I really like it and wish you would read it more often."

I also get feedback that isn't positive, but it is still important to know, like the student who told me in the reading tell-all that he pretends to read when we take out textbooks because he just doesn't know how to start.

Anecdotal Records of the Reading Conference

Anecdotal records are distinctly helpful for keeping a record of observations made while a student reads, as well as what you and students talk about during reading conferences. In the past, I always thought I would remember what I talked about with students, but sometimes I did forget. I changed my practices because having a written record meant I would never slip up.

Qualitative, holistic, quick anecdotal records are an informal way to see the big picture of your students as readers over time. Your records should include information about the students' skills in decoding, fluency, vocabulary, and comprehension. For instance, you can record if students are pronouncing the words correctly, if they are skipping or inserting words, and if the pace of their reading sounds like talking. Your notes should include information about what students like to read and what they find challenging. You can use these records to inform future conversations, plan mini-lessons, and reflect on the practice of self-selected reading. Over time, your observational comments will provide a record of reading instruction and formative assessment for each of your students.

Possible Prompts for Reading Conferences with Students

Choose from and modify this set of questions for use in your reading conferences with students in the first month of school:

- What book you are reading right now?
- What kind of book is it?
- What was your reading goal this week? (If you asked them to record a goal in their reading notebook earlier in the week.)
- Where are you in your book?
- Can you summarize what has happened so far?
- Please tell me more about …
- Why do you think …?
- How do you know …?
- What have you read so far that you have connected with?
- What themes have come up in the book so far?
- Would you please read aloud a part of the story for me?
- Have any words come up that you have difficulty pronouncing or understanding? What are they?
- What is your new reading goal as you keep reading? (Students write their new goal for reading.)

Reading Conferences Organizer

Student's Name	Current Book	Date	Comments/Observations

Pembroke Publishers ©2021 *Sometimes Reading Is Hard* by Robin Bright ISBN 978-1-55138-351-4

9. Practice Retelling with a Story Vine

I met reading consultant Marlene McKay several years ago, and she told me about her book *Story Vines and Readers Theatre: Getting Started* (2008) and the strategy of using story vines to develop students' reading skills while collaborating and contributing to meaningful classroom talk. Marlene was a travelling consultant in Northern Manitoba at the time. She told me that she shared this strategy in rural school communities as a way for children and young people to use retellings of new and traditional stories in a fun and creative way to develop the components of reading and especially fluency.

According to Marlene, story vines are based on an old African tradition of storytelling and can be used to develop language and support reading and writing across the curriculum. Story vines involve both planning and performance but are rooted in what students are reading. Students choose a story to read and represent by creating a story vine and sharing it with a group of their peers. The story vine can be shared multiple times with different audiences. This strategy

- develops students' understanding of story and sequence
- introduces students to new vocabulary
- links visual imagery with reading
- develops fluency in reading and talking

STEP BY STEP: Make a Story Vine to Develop Oral and Reading Fluency

Choose a book that you share year after year with your students, one that you love well and have almost committed to memory. In the past, I have used two of my favorite books to model this strategy, *Don't Fidget a Feather!* by Erica Silverman and *The Paper Bag Princess* by Robert Munsch. Both books have easy-to-follow, sequential story lines, engaging characters, satisfying endings, and repetitive dialogue.

Create a story vine using bunches of wool or other material to create a long braid. Then gather small toy-like artifacts that represent parts of the story and attach these like charms to the braid in an order that reflects the plot of the story. Many students create their own artifacts by finding pictures in magazines to cut out and glue to a cardboard backing or by making their own.

Read the story aloud to your students using fluent and expressive language.

Afterward, **retell the story**, using the story vine. You might say, "I would like to show you the story vine I created using this story." With enthusiasm and expression, retell the story to a group of students using the story vine and artifacts to guide you. Students may notice that the retelling is not exactly the same as the read-aloud, but they also quickly point out phrases and vocabulary that they recognize from the story. Encourage students to pick up the story vine and retell the story themselves.

After modelling the strategy, **students find stories** that they want to read and use for their story vines. Help your students use books and stories that they know well and that feature an obvious sequence, language repetition, and predictability. These characteristics support students' success with retelling. For young students I suggest stories already known to them through storytelling. Goldilocks and the Three Bears, Three Billy Goats Gruff, and even We're Going on a Lion Hunt are all good options. These stories, because many students know them already, help students with oral language fluency. Oral fluency, in turn, supports

Teaching Tip

You might consider sending a note home asking family members for donations of tiny toys or other objects. All students will benefit from having items to choose from to use on their story vines.

reading fluency, especially with English language learners and students with specific language challenges. Finding the right stories can take one or more lessons and you might want to incorporate the building of storyboards as students plan their retellings.

Students make their own braids with the assistance of a book buddy. This stage works beautifully if you bring together different age groups. Grade 5 book buddies paired with Grade 2 students, for example, works well. The Grade 5 students help their younger counterparts with the braiding and selection and creation of artifacts.

Once the story vines have been created, set aside time for students to **practice retelling their stories** using the language from the story. This can be done with the assistance of a partner (the student's book buddy), an education assistant, a parent volunteer, or you.

Once students have retold their story at least once, they **share their story vines** with small groups of peers and their families. The more opportunities students have to share their story vines with others, the more their confidence will grow in language fluency, vocabulary, and comprehension.

> Repetition is important. The more opportunities students have to share their story vines with others, the more their confidence will grow in language fluency, vocabulary, and comprehension.

Four pre-service teachers share the story vines they created to use during their practicum experiences.

Your Key Takeaways

Here are the key ideas we explored in this chapter on teaching fluency.

- Fluency refers to the accuracy, rate, and expression of reading. It is not simply the speed at which a reader reads.
- Fluency might be highlighted in reading instruction but should not be taught and measured separately from the other components of reading.

- Round-robin reading, the method of calling on students one by one to read orally, is not effective in improving fluency.
- Students need opportunities to read aloud to improve fluency but in a non-threatening atmosphere.
- Fluency builds confidence. Confidence builds fluency.
- Use students' own interest in the reading material to encourage students to read fluently and enjoy reading.
- Reading 15 minutes a day is considered a consequential length of time in helping students improve their reading skills.
- Use tools such as status-of-the-class surveys, conferences, and anecdotal comments on a regular basis as a way to monitor students' progress in reading fluency.
- Enhance fluency through collaborative reading strategies, tongue twisters, poetry, and retellings.

4

Vocabulary: Teaching How to Build a Library of Words

> **Vocabulary is the glue that holds stories, ideas and content together ... making comprehension accessible for children.**
> —*William Rupley, John Logan, and William Nichols (1998/99)*

As a teenager, I remember my dad sitting at the dining room table reading aloud from the *Reader's Digest* Word Power. Word Power was a short vocabulary quiz that appeared in every issue of the magazine. My dad would read the words out loud, often exaggerating the pronunciation and stretching the syllables. If my brother and sisters and I were in the mood, we would repeat the words after him. Then he would read three different definitions for the word and ask us to guess which one was correct. It didn't really matter which definition we chose, because he always told us the correct one and used the word in several sentences until he figured we were sure of its meaning.

I still recall learning *egregious, ineffable*, and *indignation* by listening to my dad read the quizzes from Word Power. Not exactly vocabulary for a 13-year-old! But those words were planted in my consciousness and remained there for years until I was ready to use them. That is a great way to think about what you do when you teach vocabulary: you are word planting!

> **Every time you use an interesting word that registers in a child's brain, you are word planting.**

Every time you use an interesting word that registers in a child's brain, you are word planting. And it is through words that students learn about their world and communicate with the world in return. Whether you teach seven-year-olds or seventeen-year-olds, whether you teach English language arts or dramatic arts, like every teacher of every discipline, you have a vested interest in helping students learn and expand their knowledge of words.

Language learning and all learning depends on the ability to read, understand, and use words. We know that students with robust vocabularies have strong comprehension skills and do better in school.

At the same time, however, "learning words" can be drudgery. We all know that vocabulary instruction can quickly become boring if it is not approached with motivation in mind. Have you heard your students asking, "Why do we have to do this?" I enjoyed my dad's informal vocabulary quizzes at home because, let's face it, it was just for fun.

What was language instruction like in school? I distinctly remember despising the many lists of words I had to look up in the dictionary at school. Sitting quietly at my desk along with my classmates, I looked up the list words in a dictionary, laboriously wrote out their definitions, and finally, created sentences for each word. I handed in my completed worksheet at the end of class. Done!

Keeping those early school experiences in mind, I decided that my own vocabulary instruction had to be interesting, meaningful, and collaborative. Otherwise, I knew I ran the risk of my students losing interest in reading and confidence as readers.

The Word-Rich Get Richer, The Word-Poor Get Poorer

As students begin to read in the early grades and experience success, they typically want to read more. They enjoy what has been referred to as a "rich get richer" phenomenon. Reading success leads to

- reading satisfaction
- self-confidence
- more time spent reading
- exposure to more vocabulary
- improved comprehension reading skills

Students who struggle early on in learning to read do not experience the euphoria that goes with success. Many of them experience the "poor get poorer" phenomenon. Early reading struggles lead to

- reading dissatisfaction
- lack of self-confidence
- less time spent reading
- less exposure to vocabulary
- stagnating comprehension skills

An unfortunate gap emerges between these two groups of students. And over time, it just grows. Every teacher sees this happening, and it is heartbreaking. The gap is referred to as the Matthew effect (Stanovich, 1986). This gap widens over the schooling years and has long-lasting detrimental effects.

What can you do to make a difference? One approach that bears fruit is to create a classroom where vocabulary instruction is an integral part of the day. Readers flourish when they know the meaning of the words they read. And you can make it fun.

Let's look at three effective ways to strengthen vocabulary instruction in your teaching practice.

Vocabulary is called an unconstrained reading skill because it continues to grow throughout one's life. That's good news for teachers and students alike.

1. **Expose students to reading** every day in multiple ways. Students expand their vocabulary when someone reads to them and when they read on their own.
2. **Develop your own understanding of the three tiers of vocabulary** to make decisions about words to teach across subjects and grade levels. (Words fall into one of three tiers based on frequency of use, complexity, and meaning. See pages 97–98.)

3. **Foster students' interest in and dedication to learning new words**. (By dedication, I mean the disposition to commit effort, time, and persistence to learning new words.)

Teaching Tip: *Get Your Students Using Their New Words*

Students feel motivated when they can observe their own progress. One way to help students "perceive" their growing vocabulary knowledge is simple: get them writing.

At the end of a unit such as Energy Conservation or Consumerism, ask students to write the things they learned in a paragraph or in point form. Then ask them to read their texts to one another. You might even ask them to count how many new words they learned.

After taking part in this activity, one Grade 6 student said, "I know that now I'm kind of using, like, more interesting words." Another commented, "I found interesting ... the new words that we found out. It's a way to encourage us how to use them and how to find definitions."

Continual Exposure to Reading

Vocabulary experts tell us that a reader needs at least 12 exposures to a new word before it gets incorporated into their lexicon.

In a lifetime, the average person uses between 20 000 and 35 000 words. Does anyone know how they learned those words? In most cases, it would be hard to pinpoint. Vocabulary experts tell us that a reader needs at least 12 exposures to a new word before it gets incorporated into their lexicon. One of the best ways to increase exposure to new vocabulary is through reading, both when you read aloud to students and when students read on their own or with others.

One of my colleagues, Michael Pollard, artfully read aloud Natalie Babbitt's timeless book, *Tuck Everlasting*, to a new group of pre-service teachers every fall. He knew just which words to highlight, how to project, when to whisper, and when to repeat, so that his audience could appreciate every single word in the text. Students heard vocabulary in context when Michael read aloud words such as *indomitable, melancholy, ponderous*, and *protruding*. These are words that pre-service teachers likely knew the meanings of, even if they didn't use them frequently. Exposing the audience to the words was not Michael's point, though. His point was to demonstrate how vocabulary could be taught through reading aloud.

There is just no substitute for reading aloud as a way to enrich vocabulary. Allow me to demonstrate by telling of a favorite memory of mine. Every year or two, on the eve of a new installment of the Harry Potter books, my whole family would go to our local bookstore. As we stood in line, eagerly awaiting the midnight release, we took part in games, quizzes, and activities. Then, with our copies of the book in hand, we would rush home and our daughters would devour the books.

Our eldest daughter read aloud every single Harry Potter book to her sister, who was seven years her junior. She read aloud with expression, and she gave the characters their unique voices. Her sister loved it. The benefits for both of them were immense. Together, they developed their reading skills through the simple and pleasurable act of reading aloud and listening. And the words they learned were sophisticated, interesting, and new: *muggles, snivel, apothecary, phoenix, hallows, quidditch, sorcerer*, and *basilisk*, to name a few.

The more students are exposed to reading, the more words they see and learn. This exposure is called "reading volume." As Keith Stanovich explains, "The effect of reading volume on vocabulary growth, combined with the large skill differences in reading volume, could mean that a 'rich-get-richer,' or cumulative advantage phenomenon, is almost inextricably embedded within the developmental course of reading progress" (Stanovich, 1986, p. 381).

Whether you read to your students for five minutes or twenty, the benefits to vocabulary growth are undeniable. Reading aloud helps readers figure out word meanings indirectly, so they learn them without being taught.

Which Words to Teach?

Grade school students need to learn a minimum of 2000 to 3000 words a year to be prepared for the next grade. Research says that most teachers deliberately teach around 400 new words every year. So choosing which words to teach is fraught. High-frequency words are important, but so are words associated with content-area learning.

Which words should you teach directly? Which words will you teach indirectly? Which word meanings will students pick up on their own? The decisions you make depend in large part on the texts that students will be reading. They will be of two types:

1. the texts you ask students to read
2. the texts students select to read

Students should be able to read and understand 90 to 95 percent of the words in a text that they read on their own. Otherwise, they won't get much out of what they are reading. Without understanding most of the words in a text, students will need to spend so much time on figuring out the meaning of words (and perhaps decoding them), that they will lose the gist of what they are reading. Discouragement will ensue.

Hence the need to zero in on the words that students are most likely to encounter. Isobel Beck (2002) and her colleagues categorize words into three tiers. Learning more about these vocabulary tiers will help you choose which words to teach and why.

Three Categories of Words

Tier I words

- are the most basic words found in talk and in print
- include words such as *door, table*, and *pencil*
- usually do not need to be taught because they are so common and easily recognized
- are considered to be sight words (Think of the word *stop* as it appears on the ubiquitous red, octagon sign that most of us see every day.)
- make up about 8000 words in the English language
- rarely have prefixes or suffixes

Tier II words

- are often referred to as "high-frequency words," meaning they are viewed in print regularly
- appear across subjects and grade levels (Whether you are reading a newsfeed, a story, a play, a math problem, a science textbook, or a health-and-wellness tip, these words always appear. They include words such as *similar*, *climate*, *peculiar*, and *encourage*.)
- best learned via instruction (Instruction is most helpfully focused on words in Tier II because of how frequently students will encounter them.)
- are important for comprehension
- may contain multiple meanings
- make up about 7000 word families in the English language
- can be changed with prefixes or suffixes

Tier III words

- are words that are specialized (They will be different for each grade level.)
- include words such as *igneous*, *sediment*, and *metamorphic* for Grade 3 level science
- might include *chromatography*, *endothermic*, and *polymerization* for high school chemistry
- require direct, explicit, and ongoing instruction
- are words that, in some cases, even you must look up
- are better understood when students know root words and affixes (which include both prefixes and suffixes)
- make up the remaining 400 000 words in the English language

Using the vocabulary tiers to help you decide which words to teach can pay dividends because your students will learn the words they need to be successful readers. If you are working with English language learners, they will need support learning Tier 1 words. If your students are struggling to read in science, you might want to focus on the difficult, disciplinary Tier 3 words.

Finding Books to Meet Students' Reading Needs

You wouldn't give Grade 5 students a high school textbook to read. They wouldn't get anything out of it. Similarly, if the vocabulary of any book is consistently too difficult for your students, give them another book!

For each student, a book will sit at one of three levels:

- the **independent reading level**, if students can read it on their own, easily recognizing 90 to 95 percent of the words
- the **instructional reading level**, if students can read it with some errors, but those errors do not cause frustration or problems with comprehension
- the **frustration reading level**, if students make frequent errors and those errors cause frustration and problems with comprehension

You would do well to expose your students to texts at their independent or instructional reading levels for most of the reading they do.

By getting to know your students' independent and instructional reading levels, you will be better able to expose them to books that lead to success and avoid books that lead to frustration. I should add, however, that some evidence shows that letting students struggle a little with reading is not always a bad thing. You will need to use your good judgement after observing how each of your students responds to reading difficult text, as some will stick with it and make progress while others may give up.

In My Classroom: Reading When Vocabulary Is Just Too Hard

As a pre-service teacher, I taught in a Grade 2 classroom for one of my practicum experiences. A particular memory of working with a student has never left me. One morning, I arrived at the classroom and the teacher asked me to work with Amanda, who had been away from school for the previous few days. My task was to help Amanda catch up with the reading and follow-up activities that her classmates had completed on the previous day.

Together, Amanda and I found the story that she was to read. To begin, we looked at the illustrations in the story to familiarize Amanda with the context. And then she began to read. Amanda read the first line of the story but then had trouble with several words in the second sentence—words like *string, blue,* and *people.* I employed the strategies I had learned at university, asking her to sound out the unfamiliar words and offering suggestions like, "Let's look at the three letters at the end of this word, *-ing,* to see if that helps." We also used the classroom word wall to find some words in the text. By the time we located a word and she was able to say it, though, she had lost the meaning of the sentence.

I realize now that the vocabulary in the story was simply too hard for Amanda. That does not mean that she had no reading skills; they were simply not up to the task of reading that particular story.

If I could go back, I would have spent some time teaching Amanda Tier I words, knowing they would support her in future reading. Then I would have selected a different story, perhaps even writing one of my own, for her to read, one that was more closely aligned to her level of vocabulary development and reading skills.

I cannot help wondering what effect this unsuccessful reading experience had on Amanda's confidence as a reader. It now seems like a missed opportunity to read a book with vocabulary she could read successfully.

The Role of Dedication in Vocabulary Development

Let's face it, once in a while, we all struggle with vocabulary. Being a dedicated reader can help.

Let's face it, once in a while, we all struggle with vocabulary. I have struggled to pay attention, occasionally, especially when faced with a dense, jargon-filled journal article. Reading can feel like a chore when we feel stressed about having to read something quickly, when we don't understand why we have to read something, or when we just can't get into a text right away. In all these cases, being a dedicated reader can help.

Teaching Tip

Taking the time to talk about dedication with our students as they read is key to helping them think of themselves as readers.

You may remember from Chapter 1 that dedication is one of the factors of motivation that help students want to read. Teaching students about dedication, sometimes referred to as "stick-with-it-ness," can help them keep in mind the big picture: that we all experience difficulties and we all can overcome them with a little effort (in some cases, a lot of effort). Taking the time to talk about dedication with our students as they read is key to helping them think of themselves as readers.

Today, there are countless new and trusted texts that are perfect for exploring the role of dedication in reading and in students' lives. You can use these insightful and inspiring books to spark conversations with students about reading specifically or about learning generally.

I love books that help learners recognize that they are not alone in their reading and learning struggles. Students can learn new vocabulary to help them describe how they feel when they struggle and, more importantly, how to turn those struggles around. Have a look at the following book list. I have found that books like these can encourage students to develop the dedication needed to handle reading challenges.

Best Books about Kids Who Find Reading Hard

- *Thank You, Mr. Falkner* by Patricia Polacco (ages 3–6)
- *Fish in a Tree* by Lynda Mullaly Hunt (ages 9–12)
- *The Alphabet War: A Story about Dyslexia* by Diane Burton Robb (ages 5–7)
- *Miss Malarkey Leaves No Reader Behind* by Judy Finchler (ages 4–8)
- *Leo the Late Bloomer* by Robert Kraus (ages 5–8)
- *Niagara Falls, or Does It?* by Henry Winkler and Lin Oliver (ages 9–12)

In Susan's Classroom: A Lesson in Dedication to Words

Susan teaches Grade 3, and she tells me that she and her students work together to develop their understanding of the importance of dedication when learning new words.

Susan writes the word *dedication* on the board and asks her students to think of a time when they were dedicated to something they were doing. She tells them it could be anything they had to learn, inside or outside of school.

Susan then shares an example of being dedicated to reading. She tells her students that she practices dedication to reading by trying to make time every evening to read to her own children just before bed. Sometimes she is tired, but she always reads to them anyway.

Next, she listens to what her students say about being dedicated to something and records their examples on the board using a mind map. She asks every student to contribute something and prompts those few who can't think of anything by asking questions such as, "When did you learn to tie your shoelaces?" and "How did you learn to play basketball?" and "How did you learn to ride a bike?"

Susan then reads all the responses aloud and asks the students what each of their examples has in common. Susan uses "turn and talk" with her students to give everyone a chance to participate before asking them to share their responses in the large group. Students said this about what they noticed in everyone's responses:

- "They're all things we had to learn."
- "They were hard at first but then got better [easier]."
- "They were things we like doing."
- "You have to do it a lot."
- "We had to practice to get better."
- "Yeah, we never give up."
- "We are still learning how to do it [i.e., play basketball]."

Eventually, Susan summarizes this lesson by saying, "Dedication is a habit. It is about perseverance and staying with a problem until it is solved. In this classroom, we are dedicated to learning about words to help you become even better readers. Dedication is sticking with it even when it is hard."

Finally, Susan asks students to draw and write about a real example of dedication in their lives. Their creations are displayed around the classroom for students to see and read throughout the day. She tells her students, "These stories are here to inspire you any time you are reading and something is hard for you." Developing the mindset of dedication will help students learn new vocabulary when reading becomes more complex and difficult and even, dare I say it, less interesting to them.

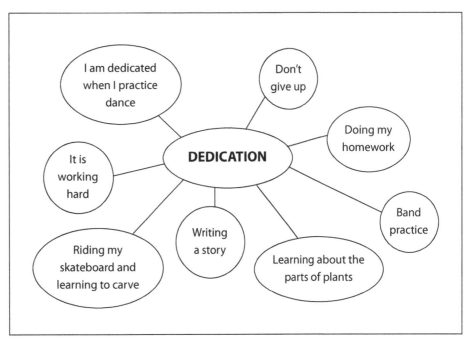

You and your students can together create a mind map to explore the role of determination in reading and other activities.

Vocabulary Instruction in Middle and High School

Research tells us that the teaching of vocabulary declines precipitously as students get older. By middle and high school, dedicated instructional time for vocabulary occupies as little as 5 percent of class time. Knowing that vocabulary remains a

We can't leave students on their own to try and make sense of increasingly challenging vocabulary as they wend their way through the grades.

key to comprehension for middle and high school students, across curriculum areas, I urge you to help counteract this decline if you work with this age group.

Vocabulary instruction for older students should always occur in the context of the reading that they do. Students encounter new words in virtually all subject areas, including English language arts, mathematics, social studies, the fine arts, physical education, informational technology, and science. Every teacher—not just language arts teachers—can ask, "What am I doing to support my students' understanding of the new words they read in my classroom?"

We can't leave students on their own to try and make sense of increasingly challenging vocabulary as they wend their way through the grades. You can provide a student-centred focus on vocabulary that is explicit, targeted, and ongoing. Identify the words that your students need to succeed and provide them with multiple opportunities to see, hear, read, and write these new words. Make sure there's time to talk about and pronounce the new words they are learning.

Engage Students with Word Games

What better way to engage students but with a game?

Students actually look forward to vocabulary practice when it takes the form of a game. Whether on paper, on a board, or in an app, games can reinforce word knowledge without being boring.

Games that can be used to reinforce and review new vocabulary include Boggle, Scattergories Junior, Pictionary, bingo, crosswords, word search puzzles, hangman, Balderdash, Blurt!, You've Been Sentenced!, and Apples to Apples. You can create versions of all these games to support the vocabulary focus you want to target. And they are all great choices for students of middle and high school age. Students might also enjoy creating and challenging each other with their own vocabulary games and activities.

Mobile devices and apps have emerged as great tools for getting students to buy in to vocabulary work. Some students can be strongly motivated to do well in digital games, so this is definitely an avenue you might explore for some students.

Here are a few well-reviewed apps that students can use on their own and with their classmates: the Root Words dictionary app, PowerVocab Word Game, Kids' Vocab—Mindsnacks, Word Hippo, Spelling City, and Wallwisher.

Key Strategies to Help You Teach Vocabulary

In the following pages of this chapter, I have gathered both new and familiar instructional strategies and practices from teachers, researchers, and my own experience. You can use them to develop students' vocabulary skills while building their motivation for reading. These eight strategies highlight vocabulary but also build capacity in the other components of reading: decoding, fluency, and comprehension.

1. Encourage word wonder
2. Teach vocabulary through a teacher read-aloud
3. Introduce vocabulary self-collection

4. Harness visualization
5. Get students playing word games
6. Galvanize a vocabulary-growth mindset
7. Preview vocabulary before independent reading
8. Build an interactive word wall

1. Encourage Word Wonder

Both my parents had what we now call "word consciousness," or a love of words. They read widely and they were writers. They shared their love of words and language with their children and, eventually, their grandchildren.

Word consciousness is an awareness that "involves an appreciation of the power of words, an understanding of why certain words are used instead of others, knowledge about the differences between spoken and written language" (Graves & Watts-Taffe, 2008). You can encourage curiosity about words simply by the example of your own enthusiasm. But you can also be very up front with students about the attitude you want them to take.

In my visits to classrooms, I have seen teachers bring the idea of word consciousness to their students in many creative ways. For instance, Grade 2 teacher Debbie and her students create bright, interactive bulletin boards with new vocabulary displayed for interactive games and activities. I can't help but smile when I hear teachers spread their enthusiasm about "amazing" words with their students, whom they grant status as word detectives, word demons, word explorers, word connoisseurs, word artists, word sleuths, or word wizards.

Lately, I have talked to teachers and students about embracing the moniker *word wonderers*. I think this phrase clinches how we want students to think about themselves in relation to vocabulary. Wondering about something often means "to be filled with curiosity and query." It is a frame of mind I observed when I taught elementary school, especially when I encouraged my students to listen to, look for, and talk about words they found interesting. When students genuinely wonder about words and language, it is exciting to see their enthusiasm and excitement.

Teaching Tip

Get excited when your students behave like they've discovered something remarkable that no one else has figured out. For them, they have!

As Gordon Wells describes, word wonderers really do "re-invent language" for themselves. As a Grade 1 teacher, I witnessed daily examples of students proudly noticing aspects of vocabulary with comments like, "I just found the word *part* in *apartment* or "Look how many little words you can make from the word *sailboat*!" Joy of vocabulary discovery is infectious, so it will be easy for you to be excited when they share these kinds of little learnings.

I still remember one of my favorite examples of word wonder when a little girl in my class exclaimed, "Did you know the word *owl* is in my bowl?" I burst out laughing. I understood and appreciated what she had just figured out about language (The word *owl* is hidden in the word *bowl*), but I also loved her thinking about an owl literally sitting in a bowl. It was amazing to see her make this discovery and know she made it. Researcher Nadia Hasan agrees, noting that "encouraging [a] discovery technique may boost up students' interest and stimulate their metacognitive awareness" (2014, p. 60). So get excited when your students behave like they've discovered something remarkable that no one else has figured out. For them, they have!

2. Teach Vocabulary through a Teacher Read-Aloud

The International Literacy Association describes read-alouds as "magic." A read-aloud is an instructional practice in which an experienced reader—the teacher in this case—reads a text aloud to students, usually in a whole-group setting.

When you read aloud to your students—and I hope you do—you increase their exposure to a wide variety of texts and vocabulary. The vocabulary in books is often richly descriptive and more varied and complex than the vocabulary of everyday conversation because it comes from literature abundant in ideas and language. Most books for children are chosen for publication because of their extraordinarily wonderful, skillful use of language. Think of Sheree Fitch's delightful book *Sleeping Dragons All Around*—the title alone conveys the exquisiteness of this author's use of language.

Vocabulary instruction may seem to come naturally to experienced teachers, but it is a skill they have developed through planning and practice. What's the secret to teaching new words through read-alouds? Here are a few hints to help you get the most out of these opportunities.

Teaching Tip

You can choose the words before reading aloud and mark them in the text with a small sticky note just as a reminder where to stop and clarify vocabulary.

1. Select a text to read aloud. It should contain rich language, have engaging content, and be appropriate for the age and interests of your students.
2. Decide on the vocabulary that needs to be taught. Typically, you would highlight Tier 2 words during a read-aloud. These are the words that tend to be less common in everyday conversation but appear frequently in written text. You can choose the words before reading aloud and mark them in the text with a small sticky note just as a reminder where to stop and clarify vocabulary.
3. Decide if you will teach the words before or during the read-aloud.
4. Choose one or more strategies to use that facilitate word learning. Several are described below.
5. Think about whether you will follow up with the vocabulary after the reading and, if so, how.

[handwritten note: have students write down words they don't know & also write words you think they won't know]

Direct and Indirect Vocabulary Instruction

Your students hear new words during read-alouds that are typically not heard in day-to-day life. While reading, pause here and there to embed vocabulary instruction. This strategy helps your students learn while interacting with the text.

I like to think of direct vocabulary instruction during read-alouds as intentional, and indirect vocabulary instruction as incidental. Books like the Fancy Nancy series by Jane O'Connor do both.

Direct vocabulary instruction. In the book *Fancy Nancy and the Fall Foliage*, the first page begins, "Fall is my favourite season. I love how the foliage changes color. (Foliage means all the leaves)." Notice how the author takes the time to directly explain what foliage means in the text. You can do the same thing when reading aloud. Stop at a word and provide an explanation or an example.

Indirect vocabulary instruction. On the next page of the book, O'Connor writes, "Mom and Dad are raking the leaves. It looks like so much fun, so I volunteer to help." As you read this sentence aloud, students learn the word *volunteer* incidentally through the reading itself—they will notice that Nancy goes outside to rake leaves. Students will learn that volunteering is about offering help, just by seeing and hearing the word used in context.

Direct and indirect vocabulary instruction are not mutually exclusive. You can use both interchangeably. Both methods let you introduce new words and phrases informally without taking away from the flow of the text.

If you are worried that embedding vocabulary instruction will take away from students' comprehension, you might consider reading a text three times: the first time to hear and understand the text, the second time to provide vocabulary and other reading instruction, and the third to enjoy and appreciate the text.

English language learners and students who struggle with reading greatly benefit from read-alouds. These students might be lost trying to read a text with unfamiliar words, idioms, or metaphors on their own. When you read aloud texts with these literary devices, you can explain words, phrases, and context that enable all students to understand and process meanings. Students can ask questions, too.

Strategies for Teaching Vocabulary During the Read-Aloud

Let's look at some of the common strategies you can use to teach vocabulary during a read-aloud. I will use one of my favorite books, *How It Was with Dooms: A True Story from Africa* by Xan Hopcraft, to illustrate. (*Dooms* is a nickname for a small male cheetah.)

The text says, "When Dooms went up on our roof, we'd try to get him down, because our roof is made of papyrus, or *marula* in the Swahili language, and papyrus is slippery and can be damaged by Doom's claws."

Here are some approaches I would use to help students understand the word *papyrus*.

- **Stop and ask a question**. When you come to the word in the text, ask "What is papyrus?"
- **Provide a definition, a synonym, or an example of the word**. "Papyrus is a kind of thick, hard grass that grows in Africa."

- **Elaborate on the word's meaning**. "In Egypt, long ago, people used papyrus for making boats, rope, sandals, and a kind of paper also called 'papyrus.'"
- **Refer to the illustrations**. Say the word and point to the illustration of papyrus on the page. "Look, here's a photo of the family's house covered in papyrus."
- **Engage students' senses**. Rub your hands together and say, "Papyrus is smooth to the touch." Many of your students will immediately copy this gesture.
- **Refer to the morphology of the word**. Depending on the age of your students, you might say, "The word *paper* traces its origin to the word *papyrus*."

When reading aloud to students, be ready to <u>take advantage of the teachable moments.</u> You know when that happens. The student sitting right in front of you points at the page, and says, "What's a jackal? That sounds weird." The time to teach that new word has presented itself.

| **In Margaret's Classroom: Teaching Vocabulary through Reading** | Listen as Grade 2 teacher Margaret reads aloud from the book *The One and Only Ivan* by Katherine Applegate and seamlessly inserts vocabulary knowledge into her reading: |

> I live in a human habitat called the Exit 8 Big Top Mall and Video Arcade …
> Mack works here at the mall. He is the boss.
> I work here too. I am the gorilla.

At this point, Margaret pauses her reading for a moment and says, "When Ivan says he lives in a human habitat, he means that he does not live in his natural home, which would be a jungle or forest, but in one created for him by people. Close your eyes and picture a natural home for a gorilla … Now picture what you think a gorilla home would look like if it was made by humans." Margaret asks a few students to describe their visualizations. They offer descriptions for a gorilla's natural home by talking about rainforests and greenery. They describe the human-made home by talking about captivity, bars, and being on display. Margaret continues to read, embedding vocabulary instruction in a brief but informative manner while reading aloud to her students.

Later, Margaret's students work in pairs. Each pair has a large piece of paper, which they fold in half. On one side, a student draws or finds images in magazines of a gorilla's natural habitat. The second student does the same on the other side of the paper to show what the gorilla's human-made habitat might look like.

Margaret encourages her students to talk to each other and to her about the images they create. Margaret's explanation of the term *habitat* has led to a fulsome exploration of an important aspect of this story: the setting. Margaret displays students' creations on a bulletin board devoted to response activities related to the book.

Read Aloud from Diverse Books for More Great Vocabulary Lessons

Diverse literature can help us to develop and extend our students' vocabulary, not to mention their imaginations, identities, and abilities to empathize.

We have many good reasons for incorporating diverse literature into our read-aloud selections (which we will explore further in Chapter 6). Besides helping us present authentic representations of varied human experiences, cultures, beliefs, and languages, diverse literature can help us to develop and extend our students' vocabulary, not to mention their imaginations, identities, and abilities to empathize.

A book like *Stepping Stones: A Refuge Family's Journey* by Margriet Ruurs provides opportunities to teach words such as *ancestors, refugee, bombs, peace, fleeing, future, battered,* and *journey*. Culture-specific books provide opportunities to learn important words from other languages, such as *tia* (Spanish for "aunt), *ami/amie* (French for "friend"), and *kokum* (Cree for "grandmother"). Here are a few more great texts to check out that bring new, diverse words into your students' vocabulary.

- *The Proudest Blue* by Ibtihaj Muhammad (ages 5–8)
- *Marcus Vega Doesn't Speak Spanish* by Pablo Cartaya (ages 10+)
- *Idriss and his Marble* by René Gouichoux (ages 5–9)
- *Habibi* by Naomi Shihab Nye (ages 12+)

3. Introduce Vocabulary Self-Collection

The vocabulary self-collection strategy (VSS) was developed by Ruddel and Shearer (2002). This small-group approach teaches vocabulary through collaboration, and we know that collaboration helps with motivation. This strategy is a great example of students working together to learn more about vocabulary and reading.

To use this approach, you and your students together choose words to learn from a text. Consequently, students learn the vocabulary in the context of a meaningful text. You can use the approach to teach vocabulary in both fiction and non-fiction texts.

. . . .

STEP BY STEP: Vocabulary Self-Collection Strategy

Teacher Omar regularly uses the vocabulary self-collection strategy (VSS) with his Grade 4 students in social studies class. Here are the steps he follows to teach vocabulary. In this example, the words are related to diversity in Alberta.

Choose a text. Omar chooses a reading from the social studies textbook, *Our Alberta* (Tyerman, BonBernard & Cardinal, 2006) to continue his students' learning about a topic he calls "Celebrating Diversity in Alberta." Students are already familiar with the textbook.

Prepare for VSS. Omar wants his students to experience the VSS before they begin reading the chapter, so he doesn't hand out the text right away. During a preparation class, Omar talks about the purpose of learning about Alberta and its cultural and geographic diversity. The students watch a video titled "Celebrating Diversity in Alberta" produced by Opportunity Alberta. After viewing the video, students brainstorm a list of vocabulary they know on this topic. Omar uses those words to make a Wordle and posts it, enlarged, in the middle of a bulletin board in the classroom.

Omar creates a wordle like this from words that his students brainstormed about diversity in Alberta. (Created at wordle.net.)

Omar always decides ahead of time how many words he wants students to find. For this text, Omar asks his students to find ten words. (He tells me that, depending on the text, he may leave it up to the students to decide on the number of words they need and want to know about before reading. The strategy can be further differentiated by limiting the number of words students find.)

Skim to find unfamiliar words. To begin, Omar asks his students to form groups of three or four. He hands out copies of the text and asks students to skim-read to find unfamiliar words. Students must take on the following roles for this task:

- **readers**: All students skim-read the text.
- **searchers**: One or two students point out words and ask the group if they would like to learn those words.
- **recorder**: One student uses a graphic organizer to record the words as they are chosen.
- **facilitator**: One student moves the group through a discussion of what each word means.

(Omar tells me that it took about a month for students to fully understand the roles he wanted them to take on and to perform them intentionally.)

Predict meaning. Whenever a word is identified and recorded (column 1), the facilitator asks each group member to predict what they think the word means. They can predict based on what they already knew about the word (column 2). They can also predict by looking at the word in the chapter and guessing its meaning based on the context (column 3).

Record all the words. In the large group, Omar asks students to share their words. He records all the words on a list on the whiteboard for everyone to see. (Omar says that the small groups often come up with the same words.)

Vocabulary Self-Collection Strategy

Students' Names: _____

Words We Want to Understand	Our Prediction		Revised Definition
	Based on what we know	*Based on the text*	
Culture	The group a person thinks they belong to	customs, art, food of a particular group	

Pembroke Publishers ©2021 *Sometimes Reading Is Hard* by Robin Bright ISBN 978-1-55138-351-4

Review the definitions. Omar and the whole class discuss all the words the groups identified. (Omar suggests that, if you do not have time to go through the words with the class, you can ask the groups to hand in their graphic organizers so that you can review them later.)

Revise the definitions. After this oral review, students then reconvene in their small groups. The student recorders, with the help of all group members, revise the group's definitions on their handout or add to them as necessary based on the oral review (column 4).

Read the text. Finally, Omar asks students to read the text, paying special attention to the identified words. (If you decide to read the chapter aloud, then you can directly and indirectly teach the words identified by the students while reading.)

....

4. Harness Visualization

By visualizing words, students can create their own pneumonic devices.

By visualizing words, students can create their own pneumonic devices to help them to remember words and their meanings. You would use this strategy primarily for content-specific vocabulary that students self-identify as challenging while reading non-fiction texts and teacher-made handouts (Robert Chesbro, 2016).

With your students, you choose words that are important to understand. They could be subject specific or general words. Students then work in pairs or groups of three to four so they can collaborate and share their learning. They explore the words using the graphic organizer that appears on the next page.

Would you like to try it? Here are the steps.

....

STEP BY STEP: In a Word, In a Symbol

Provide every student with a copy of your chosen text and the graphic organizer, below. Guide your students through these steps.

Find challenging vocabulary. Using the text that you have provided, students read the text and take time to write the words they find challenging or unfamiliar in the first column of the graphic organizer. After finishing the reading, students use the following steps to work with the words they wrote down.

Define each word. Working in pairs, students write the definition of each word in the second column by using a dictionary, drawing on their own background knowledge, or reading the word in context. In some cases, you may wish to provide definitions. It is important that students have the correct meaning of the word at this point, so you may wish to check definitions before students proceed.

Students take turns to pronounce the word.

Identify a synonym for each word. Together students talk about what could be a synonym for the word. They write that word in the third column. They can use their own background knowledge, a thesaurus, or a thesaurus website like Word Hippo to engage in this part of the strategy.

Decide on a symbol for each word. For the fourth column, students talk about and draw or describe an appropriate symbol for the word. Drawing symbols can support all students but especially English language learners who will appreciate the opportunity to think about vocabulary through pictures. Students can also share a personal connection they have with the word, if they have one.

In a Word, In a Symbol

Students' names: _____

Word	Definition	Synonym	Symbol
obtuse	means not having a point	blunt	musical symbol for B-flat: B♭

Pembroke Publishers ©2021 *Sometimes Reading Is Hard* by Robin Bright ISBN 978-1-55138-351-4

Share. Students then share their synonyms and symbols with another group of students or with the rest of the class.

. . . .

5. Get Students Playing Word Games

The strategy of making words involves making multiple words from a small set of letters, as one might do when trying to make a word while playing Scrabble. This tactile, cooperative strategy is especially good for students in middle or high school who need to understand and use increasingly complex words.

I recently worked with a group of middle school teachers who may not have been convinced that they needed to focus on vocabulary with their students. This attitude is not uncommon. A study of teachers of Grades 5, 6, and 7 showed that they devoted only 6 percent of instructional time to vocabulary. The percentage goes down to 1.4 percent in social studies, mathematics, science, and the arts (Scott, Jamieson-Noel, & Asselin, 2003).

Keep in mind that, in middle school, the need for vocabulary knowledge intensifies. While the general academic Tier 2 words students learned in elementary school were sufficient for use across content areas, that is not the case as students move up through the grades.

To help this group of teachers see the breadth of vocabulary their students had to learn over the three years they attended their middle school and the importance of helping students learn this vocabulary, I selected key words from the Grade 6 to 8 science, English language arts, mathematics, social studies, physical education, and fine arts curriculums for their district. These were all words that their students needed to know but might find hard to understand, pronounce, and spell. See the following box for a list of these words.

Word Study List

adaptation	exoskeleton	renaissance
advertisement	expression	renewable
aesthetics	glossary	resonator
algebraic	governance	rhythmic
buoyancy	humanist	solubility
Celsius	igneous	soprano
communication	irony	substance
conduction	Legislative Assembly	summarize
cooperation	lifestyle	synchronize
diagonal	locomotor	syncopation
dramatization	measurement	tensile
dynamics	metaphor	theatre
economy	microorganism	thesaurus
ecosystem	opinion	three-dimensional
emphasis	percussion	timbre
environment	performance	ukulele
erosion	photography	unison
estimate	puppetry	viscosity

When I provided this list of words to the teachers, they looked aghast at the vast amount of really tough new vocabulary their students were expected to learn when you collect them in one place. And I had provided only a small sample of vocabulary from each curriculum!

The teachers pointed out that students were not only expected to say, read, and write (spell correctly) these words. They were also expected to know their meanings and use them correctly in context. It became apparent quite quickly that the teachers needed strategies they could use daily to support their students' vocabulary development. They also discussed how beneficial it would be to work together on a school-wide, coherent plan for teaching vocabulary. Rightly so, they realized that their students' vocabulary growth would be substantially higher if they all committed to teaching vocabulary throughout the school year.

Let's have a look at how students develop their vocabulary knowledge by making words that will help them read in all content areas.

To demonstrate how to use the making-words strategy to this group of middle school teachers, I decided to focus on science vocabulary. I chose the following Grade 8 science curriculum terms: *forces, efficiency, friction, pneumatic, mechanical advantage, viscosity, salinity, hydraulic, consumption*, and *density*. Most teachers in the room were not science teachers, so they did not know all the words. Their relative unfamiliarity with these Tier 3 words was important—it allowed me to demonstrate how students might feel using the making-words strategy to learn novel or unusual new words.

You can use the same procedure with your own students using the following steps.

STEP BY STEP: Making Words

Choose words. Choose several words from the unit you are working on with your students. I suggest using 10 to 12 key concept words your students need to know.

Prepare materials. Write the words on manilla cards and then cut up each word into individual letters and place these letters into envelopes (one word per envelope). I did this for all ten words I had selected. Keep these for later.

Working with letters written on pieces of card can be liberating for students who have difficulty writing.

Teaching Tip

Wondering what word study might look like in the classroom? Have a look at the activities in three resource books: *Making Words*, *Making Big Words*, and *Making More Big Words*, all by Patricia Cunningham and Dorothy Hall. You can use these comprehensive resources to design lessons around vocabulary that are tailored perfectly for your students.

Predict meanings. Next, write the words on the whiteboard and have your students predict the meanings of the words. In this case, I asked the teachers to use the graphic organizer for the vocabulary self-collection strategy (VSS) (on page 109). The teachers predicted the meaning of the words based on their background knowledge and knowledge of word parts.

Get definitions. Next, have students find the actual definitions. The science teachers who were in attendance defined each of the words while the others checked to see how close they were in their predictions. By the end of this step, all teachers were familiar with all word definitions.

Organize groups. Organize your students into teams of four or five members and pass out the envelopes. Do not tell teams which words are in which envelopes.

Make words. Ask your students, in their teams, to make and write out as many words as they can: first 2-letter words, then 3-letter words, and so on, until they can use all the letters to make a single word. You can ask one student in each group to keep track of all words found. With my group of teachers, I also asked one of them to record the ways in which the group members talked about language and vocabulary while engaged in this activity.

. . . .

This group of middle school teachers, who taught in many content areas, quickly saw the usefulness of this activity for their students, even though the words were all science words. They noted that students would be able to manipulate, and therefore understand, patterns in words, including prefixes and suffixes. They also noted the value of having students manipulate the letters to see how the words they were using changed when letters were added or taken away. Many of the teachers said that they had always thought such activities were only appropriate for elementary school, but, once they tried it, they revised their thinking.

The teachers also talked about how using this approach to teach root words would be very helpful in a follow-up lesson on making words. For instance, one teacher said that she had not thought to teach the word *pneumatic* by focusing on its root *pneu-*, meaning "breath" or "air," until she had experienced this activity. She added that she felt that her students would understand other words they needed to read in her class by learning about root words. The teachers added that they liked the hands-on learning style of this approach.

Best Books for Vocabulary Development

Every single book has the potential to develop students' vocabulary. But some books—such as the ones in the lists below—are staples for engaging students to become what we might affectionately call "word nerds." These books introduce new and wonderful vocabulary and engage students to think about words in ways they may not have done before.

Some of these are books of poetry. Some are picture books. Every single one would make a great addition to a classroom library or teaching practice. The point of having a few of these books available in your classroom is to inspire students, not only as readers but as writers.

Books for Budding Word Nerds

Elementary
- *The Word Collector* by Peter H. Reynolds
- *The Missing Donut* (from the Big Words, Small Stories series) by Judith Henderson
- *Look! I Wrote a Book! (And You Can Too!)* by Sally Lloyd-Jones

Middle school
- *The Lost Words* by Robert Macfarlane
- *What a Wonderful Word* by Nicola Edwards
- *One Word for Kids* by Jon Gordon

High school
- *Misery Is a Smell in Your Backpack* by Harriet Ziefert
- *Beauty Is a Verb: The New Poetry of Disability* edited by Sheila Black, Jennifer Bartlett, and Michael Northen
- *Milk and Honey* by Rupi Kaur

All ages
- *When We Were Alone* by David A. Robertson (themes: Indigenous knowledge and history, social justice, strength, and empowerment)
- *Cicada* by Shaun Tan (themes: hope, perseverance, bullying, transformation)
- *How to Read a Book* by Kwame Alexander and Melissa Sweet (themes: reading enjoyment, language, poetry)

For the teacher
- *Thereby Hangs a Tale* by Charles Earle Funk
- *The Mother Tongue* by Bill Bryson
- *The Word Circus* by Richard Lederer

---

6. Galvanize a Vocabulary-Growth Mindset

When vocabulary gets hard, students may begin to think negatively about reading and they disengage. They need what Carol Dweck calls a growth mindset (2007). And this is something that you can grow in your classroom.

Students' thinking about reading sometimes falls into a negative pattern, especially when vocabulary becomes more challenging, as it does as students progress through the grades. Discouraged students say things like

- "This is harder than I thought it would be."
- "Why is this taking so long?"
- "I am getting nowhere."
- "I can't do this."

When that happens, let students know that they can counteract this negative thinking. Use the following kinds of language with students to help change their thinking about reading challenges:

- "I'm glad you're willing to try this even though you aren't sure how to start."

Teacher Marina uses a fabulous quote in her Grade 8 classroom when she notices a student becoming frustrated with a reading task: "If something doesn't challenge you, then it doesn't change you."

- "You are learning you need to pick 'just right' books for yourself."
- "Look how close you were to reading that word."
- "You might not be able to read this yet, but you will be able to soon."
- "You reread that sentence when it didn't make sense. What a great strategy."
- "I know that you can do this."
- "Let's find out together."

Encourage students to change their language. These kinds of self-talk statements motivate them to tackle difficult vocabulary:

- "I dedicate myself to the task when things get tough."
- "Every problem has a solution, and I can figure this out."
- "I can ask for help if I get stuck."
- "Every day, I am getting to be a better reader. This is just a temporary setback."
- "Think. What is best for me to do now?"

Tackling Unfamiliar Words

Every reader confronts and masters difficult vocabulary at some point in their reading lives. I have a vested interest in reading on topics related to language and literacy, so I don't give up on unfamiliar words when they appear in a jargon-filled journal article. I stick with the task of trying to figure the words out by looking for context clues, rereading the passage, or looking them up on a word app.

In part, my interest keeps me trying to understand difficult language. But I also have a growth mindset: I'm determined to figure out those tough words. And my mindset works because I have tools—strategies—to help me tackle those words.

Your students will embrace a growth mindset if you give them the tools they need to figure out words on the fly while they read. They need to know not only what a word means but also how to pronounce it. Pronunciation is almost as important as meaning. You want students to feel confident about saying words aloud as they read. Too many students grow up not feeling confident saying new words when they encounter them. This means that some new words don't really become part of their spoken vocabulary unless and until they take the time later to note the correct pronunciation.

Using the Step by Step feature below, you can model for your students three help-myself strategies to use when they come to an unfamiliar word.

For your demonstration, choose a text on a topic that will interest your students and that includes vocabulary you want them to learn. The text can be fiction or non-fiction. In middle and high school, you might consider using a text from outside your area of expertise so that it contains vocabulary that genuinely stumps you as well as your students.

For older students, I would suggest *Botanicum* by Kathy Willis (ages 10+), *5,000 Awesome Facts (About Everything!)* from National Geographic Kids (ages 8–12), or *Stamped: Racism, Antiracism, and You* by Jason Reynolds and Ibram X. Kendi (ages 12+).

Too many students grow up not feeling confident saying new words when they encounter them. This means that some new words don't really become part of their spoken vocabulary.

Teaching Three Help-Myself Word Strategies

Choose a text. I chose the lovely picture book, *Stellaluna* by Janell Cannon, for a read-aloud with a Grade 2 class studying bats. The read-aloud demonstrates three word strategies: sound-it-out, read-it-again, and make-connections.

Prepare. Read through the text and find the vocabulary you wish to bring to students' attention: words they need to know to understand what they are reading. Use sticky notes to mark the words.

Figure out how you will ensure that students can see the text. Use a big book (for the younger grades), a document projector, or multiple copies of the text for students to share.

Create a three-column graphic organizer on chart paper for demonstration purposes and place it alongside the text so that the students can see it. Here are the column headings:

Help-Myself Word Strategies

Word	Help-Myself Word Strategies	Results

Introduce a strategy. Tell students you are going to teach them three new word strategies to use when reading. "Today I am going to use three help-myself word strategies to show what readers do—and what you can do—when facing an unfamiliar word." Add, "They are called 'help-myself word strategies' because you can use them yourself to figure out a new word. Let's see how it works."

Begin reading. Read aloud from the book, *Stellaluna*. Help-myself word strategies can be used at any point in the book, but this demonstration begins when you come to the following sentence:

> But Stellaluna had flown far ahead and was nowhere to be seen. The three anxious birds went home without her.

Identify a tough word. Read the first sentence and begin the second but pause before reading the word, *anxious* and point to it. You might say, "Okay, this word looks unfamiliar to me ..." Then, point to the three-column graphic organizer and add, "... so I am going to write it down here to look at it more closely." Write "anxious" in the first column under the title, "Word."

Sound-it-out word strategy. Begin by decoding:

- Say, "I am going to use a help-myself strategy here: the sound-it-out strategy! Let me use my decoding (sounding-out) skills to see if they will help me when I hear the word."
- Write "sound it out" in the column labelled "Help-Myself Word Strategies."
- Sound out the letters slowly and one at a time so that students can make the letter-sound correspondences with you: "/a/ /ng/ /k/ /SH/ /i/ /u/ /o/ /s/." When you get to the last four letters, sound them out as individual sounds—because that is what your students would do.

At this point, be prepared for a student to put up a hand and pronounce the word correctly. If so, say, "Well done! That's it, I think." It is likely that this student or others will be able to define it now that they have heard it pronounced correctly. That's okay. They have just prepared your other students for what is to come!

If some students do appear to understand the word, you can say, "Let's try another help-myself word strategy or two just to make sure we are correct about what this word is and what it means."

Before proceeding, say, "This sound-it-out word strategy helped me with the first part of this word but not the second part. And it did help __ [name of student]." In the third column of the chart, put a ✓ and an X to show that the strategy worked for one student but not for you.

Read-it-again word strategy. Moving on, say, "Let's try another strategy." The students might offer suggestions, or you might say, "I am going to reread these two sentences and see if that helps figure out the word." Then write, "read it again" in the middle column in the chart.

When you reread the sentence, begin to pronounce the word by saying /a/ /ng/ /k/ and you will probably hear expressions of agreement that /a/ /ng/ /k/ /SH/ /i/ /s/ is the correct way to read this word. Ask your students what the word means. They will probably say it means worried or concerned. Make a check mark in the third column and say, "It helped me to sound it out and reread the sentence to figure out what the word is, didn't it?"

Make-connections word strategy. While the first two help-myself strategies may have helped your students to recognize and say the word *anxious*—and understand its meaning—you can use your more extensive language knowledge to support their vocabulary development even further with one more strategy:

- Write "make connections" in the second column under "Help-Myself Word Strategies."
- Say, "I am going to connect this new word with other words I know that look like it. This is going to help me say the word correctly."
- Write other words that end in *-ious* in the third column of the chart, saying, "Here are other words I know that end with *-ious*. For example, write "curious." Pronounce it slowly and ask students to say it with you once, twice, three times. Say, "I know that when I see the letters *ious* together, it is sounded like this: /i/ /s/."
- Then say something like, "Let's look at the unfamiliar word again and this time, let's remember that it ends the same way as the word *curious*."

Continue to read the story and use the help-myself word strategies when needed, but not at the expense of students understanding the whole story or section of text you are reading. When you use one or more of these strategies on a first read-through of a text, limit your instruction to only a few words. You don't want to run the risk of losing the story line.

Reflect. At the end, review the steps taken and refer to the three-column graphic organizer as you do this. Ask students to read the words they learned about during the reading. Ask for their pronunciations and meanings. Then, review the steps taken for each of the word strategies used: 1) sound-it-out, 2) read-it-again, and 3) make-connections.

Prepare for independence. Ask students, "What would you do if none of these help-myself strategies helped you figure out this word?" Encourage them to recognize that the dictionary is a resource that can help with word meanings,

Using Help-Myself Word Strategies

Student name: _____

Help-myself word strategies I can use:
- sound it out
- read it again
- find a connection

Word	Help-Myself Word Strategies		Result
anxious	sound out reread	connections	X or Y

Pembroke Publishers ©2021 *Sometimes Reading Is Hard* by Robin Bright ISBN 978-1-55138-351-4

either the big ol' hard copy available in classrooms or online versions. Students might have other ideas as well, such as asking a friend or parent. The important thing is that they take action, and don't just skip over the unfamiliar word.

Let them try it. Hand out to students a copy of the graphic organizer on the previous page and ask them to use it with another text that you provide or that they are reading on their own. Make copies of this organizer easily accessible to students to use any time they are reading. When you see your students using this strategy on their own, you will know that they are attempting to understand unfamiliar words while they read!

. . . .

7. Preview Vocabulary before Independent Reading

Classrooms are very busy places. You probably have little choice but to switch from one subject to the next with little time in between to take a breath. Many students feel frustrated, though, when they must dive into a text without support.

In Chapter 3, we saw how important vocabulary preparation is for oral reading. Previewing a text for vocabulary is equally beneficial before students read independently, but only when you manage it in a meaningful, interesting, and engaging way. Giving students advance understanding of difficult vocabulary is one of the most valuable things you can do for your students.

Previewing before students read gives you the chance to intervene on your students' behalf to make sure that they have a successful and appropriately challenging reading experience. If you know your students' reading abilities, you will know what words they will find challenging, so you can tailor your preview. This will help them pull the main ideas from their reading as well as learn new words in the texts.

I now know that this was the step that was missing when I worked with Amanda in my student teaching experience. Had I previewed the text and known more about Amanda's reading abilities, I could have used a different text with her and helped teach vocabulary from the story to aid comprehension. If you are unsure whether a text is a good fit for vocabulary teaching, try the following Step by Step feature to preview a text.

. . . .

STEP BY STEP: How to Preview

Whenever possible, take time to read the text beforehand, whether it is a picture book, a chapter book, a textbook, a play, or any piece of writing that students will read. Ask yourself which of your students will read this text …

… at the level of independence?
… at the level of instruction?
… at the level of frustration?
(For definitions of these levels, see page 98.)

The students who will read at an independent level can read the text either on their own or with other students. The students who will be at their frustration level will need additional supports. Perhaps they will need to read with a partner, listen to the passage being read on tape, or have a different text altogether. For most students, the text will likely be at their instructional level. These are the students who will benefit most from the previewing strategy.

Identify vocabulary words. Look for words in the text that will be challenging for many students. Create a list of these words. Here is a teacher's list of vocabulary for a text her Grade 3 students will be reading in a science unit on plants.

Teacher's Vocabulary List for Chapter on Plants

1. seedlings	7. flower
2. mature	8. leaves
3. pollination	9. fertilization
4. sprout	10. stamen
5. stem	11. chlorophyll
6. roots	12. stigma

Teaching Tip

Designate students in your classroom as Preview Reading Experts (PREs) at different times and with different texts throughout the school year. All students should have a turn taking on this role. They learn to seek out vocabulary words by reading headings and chapter titles, looking for bold and italicized words, and scanning for words that might be challenging when they and their classmates read the text. Students take this job seriously knowing they are helping their classmates learn new words.

Decide how to handle vocabulary. Circle the words that could be taught *before* the students read a chapter in their science textbooks and underline the words that students are able to learn *through the context* of the reading. (You could record additional words that may cause problems for certain students but not all of them. Check in with those students to support their understanding of those terms during the reading.)

Alternative: Share the previewing role. You can share the previewing role with your students. It's like being asked to be the teacher! Designate different students at different times as preview reading experts (PREs), so that all students play this role in the classroom at different times in the school year (see Teaching Tip at left). Like you, the PREs preview the chapter or an excerpt from it and make a list of the words that are hard for them.

Compare the PRE's lists with your own to get a sense of how much vocabulary work, if any, needs to be done to support students as they read the text.

Compile a list of words drawn from both your list and the students' lists, including words that are challenging but also words that are central to understanding what is read. Now let's see how to use the vocabulary list you and your PREs created.

· ·

STEP BY STEP: Use Direct and Indirect Vocabulary Instruction

Prepare: Create a two-column organizer with the headings "Words" and "What They Mean." There should be room for students to write the definitions beside the words. In it, list the "hard" words. Create enough copies for all students.

Provide the vocabulary list. Before students start reading, give all of them a copy of the graphic organizer. With older students, you can simply dictate the words.

Introduce the words. Read the words aloud and ask students to repeat them together to learn and practice their pronunciation. Tell students how the list was created and ask them to watch for these words as they are read.

Highlight the words. It is helpful if students have permission to highlight the words when they find them in the text.

Direct instruction. Some of these words will be taught through direct instruction and some through indirect instruction. Direct instruction takes place first, for all words that need to be defined *before* reading, either because they are integral to understanding main ideas or because the students do not have the background knowledge to make sense of them. Draw students' attention to these words on the graphic organizer. Provide definitions to students orally and have students record these in the second column, entitled "What it Means."

Indirect instruction. Tell students that the other words on their list can be figured out as they read. Ask them to look for these words while reading and to write their own definitions on their graphic organizers. As much as possible, keep the words to five on a page so that they don't get bogged down and lose the fluency they need to comprehend the text. This number is somewhat arbitrary; use your own judgement about exactly how many words to choose. Let the length and complexity of the text guide you.

Debrief. After the reading, talk with students about both the content and the vocabulary of the reading. Ask students to share their definitions of the vocabulary that you wanted them to learn through the context as they read the text. When calling on individual students to share their definitions, you can use a "thumbs up, thumbs down," to check student understanding of the vocabulary. Have students modify their own written definitions if necessary.

Encourage students to use the graphic organizer any time they read. When you see your students using this strategy on their own, you will know that they are on their way to successfully monitoring their strategy use as readers!

· ·

8. Build an Interactive Word Wall

I remember visiting *Le mur des je t'aime* (in English, the *Wall of Love*) in a leafy green square in Paris. The phrase "I love you" appears more than 300 times in some 250 languages on a tiled, dark blue wall. It is quite a sight watching people from all over the world take photos, hold hands, kiss, and look for the letters of the phrase "I love you" in their own language.

The *Wall of Love* gives us a beautiful, rich experience celebrating three simple words. As a teacher gazing at this work of art, I could not help but think of the many word walls I have encountered in classrooms over the years. They also celebrate words.

Word walls are vibrant, colorful places in the classroom, where new vocabulary is displayed and organized underneath the letters of the alphabet. Students add to it and teachers use it for all types of word activities. Quite simply, it is a strategy used to teach and review vocabulary to increase fluency and develop comprehension.

The very best word walls are those that students help to create and then use throughout the day in an interactive way. In these classrooms, word walls are at eye level of students and are easily accessible. Students often scan the word walls from their desks. When students are coaxed to use their word wall, they will run

The very best word walls are those that students help to create and then use throughout the day in an interactive way.

up to it to look for words. They add words. They remove words, too, peeling the words off Velcro fasteners to take back to their desks and use for writing. You can encourage the interactive use of a word wall by using it to play letter and word games or practice alphabetization. You can even have students create symbols and pictures to accompany the words.

STEP BY STEP: ## How to Build a Word Wall

Start small. Build the wall incrementally. Make it something you do together; students should be included in the creation of a word wall, not see it already completed when they walk into the classroom. If your students were to enter your classroom and see a word wall already full, they would likely be overwhelmed. When this happens, the word wall becomes a classroom decoration rather than a helpful, interactive teaching tool.

Make a plan of rotation. To rotate words on the word wall selectively, first consider which words your students will need at the beginning of the year, as the year progresses (as new concepts are introduced), and then near the end of the year. This strategy will help you know how to grow the word wall and how to maintain it.

Demonstrate. Show students how to use the word wall interactively. Encourage them to take words off the wall and use them in their writing, to play games, and to write them into their own personal dictionaries. Students should help you add new words as needed.

Add words. Try to avoid teaching word wall words in isolation of the real reading that students do. Rather, words should be taught when students encounter them in a text. Where possible, engage students' decoding skills.

> If your students were to enter your classroom and see a word wall already full, they would likely be overwhelmed. When this happens, the word wall becomes a classroom decoration rather than a helpful, interactive teaching tool.

Words for Word Walls

What words should you add to word walls? This is going to vary depending on the grade level and subject areas that you teach. In elementary school, I suggest drawing from the following:

- students' names
- high-frequency words such as those found on the Fry and Dolch lists of words
- sight words
- community-based words
- content-specific words
- words with onsets and rimes that students can use to learn new words easily (such as /b/ /ack/, /m/ /ight/, and /g/ /ate/).

In middle school and high school, you might use the following:

- students' names
- root words
- content-specific words
- words from students' independent reading
- thematic and topical words

- literary terms
- words of the day
- second language words

Text structures are used in non-fiction text. It is helpful for students to know the words and phrases that signal these structures.

Text Structure	Text-Structure Word
description	*for example*
sequence	*to begin with, initially*
cause and effect	*therefore, consequently*
compare and contrast	*different from, likewise*
problem and solution	*evidence is*

Teaching Tip: *Word Walls for All Grades*

Word walls are a fixture in many elementary classrooms, but they appear less frequently in middle and high school. Why not? Since when does vocabulary stop being important to learning? Never. Research points out that middle-level and secondary students also deserve print-rich classroom environments, which can boost learning across disciplines. For example, Janis Harmon and her colleagues suggest that language arts teachers of *any* grade display words that are challenging to spell. Mathematics teachers can use word walls to introduce new words and concepts and to illustrate mathematical symbols, and social studies teachers can categorize important historical terms to help students remember.

Try These Word Wall Activities

Once you have established the word wall in your classroom, make sure you and your students make the most of it! A few of my favorite word wall activities are described below.

Word bingo. Students create bingo cards using a select number of words from the word wall. You or a student reads word definitions. Students with cards cross out the corresponding word on their cards until someone wins.

Word search. Students create word searches and then trade these to solve the puzzles made by other students.

Words within words. In groups, students choose words from the word wall. Using the "making words" strategy described earlier in this chapter (pages 113–114), they write the word on a piece of heavy paper. Then they cut the word into individual letters. (Try to make sure each group has words that are similar in length. For instance, start with five-letter words and then increase the number of letters over time.) Students make as many 2-, 3-, 4-, and 5-letter words as possible within a set time. The group with the most words wins.

Alphabetization games. Each student chooses a word from the word wall. Number the students off into groups of varying numbers. Students then have one minute to arrange themselves into the alphabetical order of their words. You can start by having students in small groups, of possibly four students per group. Then, as the game progresses, slowly make the groups larger until everyone in the class must arrange their words—and therefore themselves—alphabetically.

Six-word stories. Students choose six words from the word wall and then use them to create a story.

Found poetry. Students choose as many words as they want to create a poem. The qualification is that they cannot use any words that are not on the word wall. You may wish to put a time limit on the activity.

Word sneak. Students work in pairs. The partners take turns choosing a set number of words from the word wall, while the other partner keeps their eyes closed. To begin, each student should have a pile of five or six word cards in front of them, turned upside down. Student 1 picks up a card and peaks at it. Student 1 begins talking about anything at all, but while talking, they "sneak" the word they are holding into the conversation. After Student 1 uses the word in the conversation, they can put it down in a pile. Student 2 picks up a word card from their pile and keeps the conversation going trying to sneak *their* word in. The partners keep going, taking turns until all the word cards have been used or one of the students is stumped and cannot keep the conversation going. This works best with an audience—and it can be very funny! Students will sometimes ask you or another student to choose the word cards, which means they really must improvise.

In David's Classroom: Word Walls in Math Class? Of Course!

David is a veteran Grade 7 mathematics teacher in a busy inner-city middle school where I often visit pre-service teachers during their practicums. On my way into the school, David popped by and indicated that, if I had time, he would like me to see his math word wall.

I was intrigued and interested. I had, for years, taught pre-service teachers about the value and importance of word walls in elementary school, in English language learning, and in English language arts classrooms, and had only recently begun talking about their role in other disciplines and at higher grade levels.

As David told me later, he had noticed that his students' achievement in mathematics was being affected by their reading levels. At the time, he did not consider himself a teacher of reading. That all changed.

It changed because, after David started using strategies associated with teaching vocabulary in mathematics class, he noticed his students were more engaged in learning. They were achieving better marks in class, too.

One of the strategies David used was the word wall. It was simple. He created an easy-to-access bulletin board, formatted according to the alphabet with word cards arranged underneath each letter of the alphabet. It featured vocabulary his students were learning in a unit on geometry.

While I was used to seeing word walls in elementary classrooms, it was exciting to see one in a Grade 7 mathematics classroom.

While I was used to seeing these in elementary classrooms, it was exciting to see it in a Grade 7 mathematics classroom with vocabulary such as *perimeter, trapezoid, radius, cylinder, circumference, parallelogram, diameter*, and many others, all posted under the appropriate letter of the alphabet alongside visual aids and definitions.

I observed David using the word wall regularly during instruction, adding new words as students encountered them in the textbook, focusing on the spelling of these new words, and teaching students how to associate them with images and their meanings. He tells me that the word wall gives his students more independence, since they can refer to it anytime in class. He says it is a great support for all students but especially to English language learners and kids who are sometimes just nervous about math vocabulary.

Your Key Takeaways

Here are the key ideas explored in this chapter on teaching vocabulary.

- Like every teacher of every discipline, you have a vested interest in helping students learn and expand their vocabulary.
- Vocabulary is called an unconstrained reading skill because it continues to grow throughout one's life.
- All students, regardless of age, require a student-centred instructional focus on vocabulary that is explicit, targeted, and ongoing.
- Students expand their vocabulary when they read.
- You can use your knowledge of the three tiers of vocabulary to inform your teaching across subjects and grade levels.
- Developing the habit of dedication helps students to learn new vocabulary when reading becomes more complex and difficult.
- Students' interest in reading is boosted when they genuinely wonder about words. Their efforts are rewarded when you get excited about their discoveries.
- You can employ strategies that teach new words intentionally (using direct instruction) and incidentally (using indirect instruction).
- Students of all ages deserve print-rich classroom environments, which can boost learning across disciplines.

5

Comprehension: Teaching How to Construct Meaning from Reading

> Good comprehension instruction includes both explicit instruction in specific comprehension strategies and a great deal of time and opportunity for actual reading, writing, and discussion of text.
>
> —Nell Duke and P. David Pearson, (2008/2009)

So, here we are. Decoding, fluency, and vocabulary all take readers along the pathway toward comprehension—the ultimate goal of reading. When you weave these reading skills together with factors of motivation, it is true, to quote Aristotle, that "the whole is greater than the sum of its parts." Our students experience what, as you may recall, Nancy Frey calls, "the thrill of comprehension."

You know that students are experiencing the thrill of comprehension when a high school student thanks you for suggesting she read a novel by Julie Murphy, saying, "That book gave me all the feels." Or when a student who read the book *Wishtree* by Katherine Applegate says, "It is the first time I have ever seen myself as the hero in a book instead of the villain!" Or when you have a conversation like this with a nine-year-old:

> **Teacher**: What book did you read this month?
> **Student**: I read … I *really* liked … Captain Underpants.
> **Teacher**: I saw you reading that book! Why did you like it?
> **Student**: Because before … I didn't like reading. But then, I could read this book. The whole thing. I didn't need any help. And it's so funny!

When successful, reading is a beautiful negotiation between the reader and the text.

Comments like these from students show us ways that reading is revelatory. Reading involves the ability to understand and interpret printed text. When successful, reading is a beautiful negotiation between the reader and the text. The result *is* thrilling! We feel accomplishment, power, and joy when we comprehend and connect with what we read.

And so we should. Maryanne Wolf, author of *Reader, Come Home* sheds light on the cognitive and emotional responses engaged in the brain when one reads. Reading, she says, is like "what goes on in the multiple acts of a three-ring circus. But in our reading circus, there will be five rings with ensembles of fantastically dressed performers at the ready to act out the gamut of processes necessary to read a single word." (2018, p. 21). Comprehension is a big deal.

This doesn't happen easily for all of our students. We now know that if the prerequisite skills in the reading components—decoding, fluency, and vocabulary—are not continually being reinforced, many students will struggle with comprehension.

So what can you do to help the students in your classroom who find that comprehension eludes them? You can continue to provide instruction in the three reading components covered thus far, knowing that these will take your students far along the pathway toward comprehension. At the same time, you can build confidence in students by reassuring them that you are there to help. And, equally important, you can teach your students strategies to help develop their reading comprehension.

How to Foster Comprehension

- Discuss the purpose: Why are you reading a particular text with students (or asking them to read it)?
- Ask students to make personal connections not only with literary texts but also with factual texts.
- Build students' background knowledge about the reading topics.
- Engage students in discussion and informed debate, inviting them to express themselves but also to listen to their peers' connections with the text and their interpretations.
- Validate multiple perspectives.
- Teach the strategies that good readers use, with comprehension being the ultimate goal.
- Integrate complementary information from other media.
- Support students who want to build up their comprehension through some form of action—write a story, compose a song, create and defend an argument, work on a service project, or research an historical figure.

Why Comprehension Is Sometimes Hard

Students who struggle with comprehension are not lazy or unmotivated. They are likely working ridiculously hard but with little success. And that is frustrating! I remember Jeremy, a young student I taught in Grade 1, who tried hard to memorize everything he read because he thought that was what he was supposed to do when reading. Jeremy was unable to keep the main idea of what he was reading in his mind because he was constantly trying to remember every little detail. This made comprehension hard for him.

Only after I had figured out what was behind Jeremy's lack of comprehension could I help him. So the first thing you should try to figure out is *why* certain students do not comprehend what they are reading. As we have seen in previous chapters, there is always a reason that students struggle. They may work hard to sound out words and then lose the meaning of the sentence or paragraph. They may have a small sight-word vocabulary, which compromises fluency. Perhaps they can read each individual word on a page but are unable to put the words together. They may find the reading they do boring and uninteresting. Or they may simply avoid reading because of bad associations, so they never progress.

Recognizing When Comprehension Is Lagging

Normally, comprehension is impeded because of a combination of skill and motivation factors. Here's what students might say when comprehension is hard:

- "It takes me so long to read."
- "I can't remember what I read."
- "I get tired while reading."
- "I don't know what to do when I can't read a word."
- "I don't know what it is about."

Use the observation chart shown on the next page to help you identify and document behaviors typical of students who struggle with comprehension.

Comprehension: An Interactive Personal Experience

Reading is a transactive process in which a reader negotiates meaning in order to comprehend or create an interpretation.
—Louise Rosenblatt, 1978

Comprehension is not only about what's going on *in the text*, it is also about what's going on *in the head*. This reminds us that the skills students bring to the act of reading matter, but so too do their individual attributes.

The significance of the differences among the unique experiences of students cannot be overlooked in comprehension. Every student brings a unique set of feelings, associations, background knowledge, and motivations to reading. Differences among students explain why reading instruction that follows a set of carefully planned procedures never yields the same result for all students. This is especially true in relation to comprehension.

Each reader must critically engage with the content to derive meaning from it. For example, the student who has arrived in your classroom from Syria and the student born in North America will bring different feelings, memories, and ideas to a book like *My Beautiful Birds* by Suzanne Del Rizzo, a story about a Syrian boy whose family is forced to flee their home for the safety of a refugee camp.

When you are aware of the importance of what the learner brings to comprehension, you can better plan your instruction to recognize and take advantage of what your students bring to the table.

- Invite response and discussion from your students.
- Encourage talk among students that respects their various points of view.
- Support students to seek deeper meanings than they might do on their own.
- Help students connect new texts and experiences with those previously encountered.

Behaviors to Look for When Students Struggle with Comprehension

Student's name: _____ Date: _____

OBSERVATIONS	Always	Sometimes	Never
The student has trouble being able to tell someone the main ideas of what they read, but they can remember small details from the story.			
The student reads the words correctly and fluently but then cannot tell someone what they read.			
The student rushes through reading to get it done.			
The student finds it hard to answer "why" questions regarding what they read. (For example, Why did the main character act the way he did?)			
The student finds it difficult to connect events in a story or in informational text.			
The student appears uninterested in reading the text.			
The student looks for ways to avoid reading.			
The student finds it hard to explain how a character is feeling or what a character is thinking.			
The student appears to lack concentration.			

Pembroke Publishers ©2021 *Sometimes Reading Is Hard* by Robin Bright ISBN 978-1-55138-351-4

Creating a Mindset Primed for Comprehension

We discovered in Chapter 3 that confidence plays a role in developing fluency, and it matters with comprehension, too. Think about how you learned to read. If you're lucky, you might have early memories of a parent, grandparent, or maybe a favorite teacher helping you to read. Perhaps they helped you develop positive feelings about reading, and thoughts of "I can do this." Maryanne Wolf tells us that it is interacting with another person while learning about books and words that helps motivate both learning to read and loving to read.

Levels of self-confidence, motivation, and comprehension all feed into the other two.

Does the above cycle look familiar? If children don't feel confident as readers because of their skill level, their comprehension suffers and their motivation takes a hit. If children don't comprehend what they read, their motivation to read drops and then their confidence suffers.

We cannot allow self-confidence to be crushed as six-, seven-, or eight-year-old students are trying to learn to read. Or as older students strive to cope with increasingly difficult texts. I want to stress again how important it is to tell students you believe in them and that they will learn to master the skills they need to read successfully. Comprehension depends on good instruction, that's true. But a supportive classroom context that builds confidence must also be present. Otherwise, according to experts, "the comprehension instruction will not take hold and flourish" (Duke & Pearson, 2008/2009, p. 108). You must *believe* in them so that they will believe in themselves.

With all this in mind, you can see why a crucial role of the teacher is to boost students' confidence that they will be able to understand what they read, even when it's not happening yet. Students' levels of confidence affect whether and how they will use the comprehension instruction you provide.

Mike is a teacher who takes the time to reassure students that they do not have to read perfectly. He also emphasizes the usefulness of students supporting one another in the classroom. Mike knows that there are readers of varying abilities in his classroom. He wants them all to know that they will learn to use strategies that lead to comprehension of texts they read both in and outside of school.

In Mike's Classroom: Right Where You Should Be

Students in Mike's Grade 5 classroom are well aware of his belief in them. He speaks to all his students to inspire them. He knows that this is essential to help them persevere to the point that they reap the reward of comprehending the text that they read. Notice how frank Mike is with his students:

> You are right where *you* need to be as a reader when you came into this classroom. You do not need to be a perfect reader here—no one is. Did you know that good readers make mistakes? They do. I do. That is how they learn to become better readers. Our job in this classroom is to work together to help everyone improve their reading skills over the school year. We can do that by learning about good reader strategies and by being kind and respectful toward each other as we read and make mistakes. We celebrate each other as we improve as readers.

Mike tells his students that they are "right where they should be" as readers, and that they are part of a reading community. His students know that they are not alone in their struggles or their successes as readers.

Nothing replaces the attention and care that students feel through whole-group and one-on-one talk about reading with their teacher. You can provide your students with a rich repertoire of effective comprehension strategies but also the confidence to use them.

Three Stages of Reading: Three Opportunities to Boost Comprehension

Reading begins even before the book is opened. You can think of it as a process with three stages: 1) before reading, 2) during reading, and 3) after reading. That means you have three opportunities to boost the likelihood that your students will fully comprehend what they read. Ask yourself the following questions before having students read:

- What support do my students need *before* they read to better understand this text?
- What support do my students need *while* they read to better understand this text?
- What support do my students need *after* they read to better understand this text?

Teaching Tip

Engage your students at all three stages of the reading process to them a better chance of comprehending and connecting with a textbook reading.

Let's have a look at an example of how you might use the reading stages to improve comprehension in a social studies class. Perhaps you decide to teach about local government. You could ask students to turn to a particular chapter in the textbook and read the information therein to learn about local government. That might work for a few students. But you could also engage your students at all three stages of the reading process, giving them a better chance of comprehending and connecting with the textbook reading.

How You Could Take Advantage of the Three Stages of Reading to Teach Local Government

Before reading

- Take your students on a field trip to your local city hall to tour city chambers, departments, and offices and to meet with government representatives who tell students about their jobs.
- Give your students a reason for reading the textbook. For example, ask them to think about the information they learned about local government on their field trip and compare it with what they read in their text.
- Show your students an enlarged copy of a Venn diagram to compare the information they learn from the fieldtrip with the information from the textbook. Tell them that after the reading, you will record their findings on it.

During reading

- Ask your students to read with a partner, using one of the student-led reading strategies described in chapter 3.
- Direct students to make notes as they read. They can make notes about how the information in the text is the same or different from that they learned on their field trip to city hall.

After reading

- Lead a discussion of your students' findings, and record their observations on the enlarged Venn diagram. Use the graphic organizer to compare the information they gathered from the two sources. Information that they gathered from both places can be recorded where the two circles of the Venn diagram intersect.

This is just one example showing how you can take advantage of the three stages of the reading process to support student comprehension in your classroom. I hope you will find other examples in your own teaching practice.

In Melissa's Classroom: Before Reading, During Reading, and After Reading

Melissa's Grade 2 students are about to read about a character named Brian in the book, *The Invisible Boy* by Trudy Ludwig. Here are a few of the strategies Melissa tells me she will choose from to help students to develop their comprehension skills during this reading experience.

Before reading
- Students take part in a think-pair-share activity to respond to these questions:
  - "What does invisible mean?"
  - "Have you ever felt invisible? What did you do?"
- Melissa shows her students the book cover and reads the title. She reads the first line of the story: "Can you see Brian, the invisible boy?" She asks her students to predict what the story will be about.
- Melissa creates a character map on chart paper with the name *Brian* in the middle. She tells students they will work together to add words to describe the main character as she reads the story.

During reading
- Melissa pauses at various times while reading, asking students for the words they want her to write on the character map. Students make suggestions, she jots them down, and then the reading continues.
- Melissa stops reading at one point in the story, and asks, "How do you think that made Brian feel?" She asks the same question at the very end of the story.
- Melissa asks, "What do you notice about how the illustrator has drawn the characters in this story? Why might the illustrator do that?"

After reading
- Melissa asks students to talk about how the book made them feel. She responds positively to what they share.
- Melissa asks her students if they have ever had experiences similar to Brian's, and invites them to share.
- She then asks students to summarize the story in three parts: beginning, middle, and ending.
- The students write an exit slip responding to this question: "What would you like to ask or say to the author or illustrator of this book?"
- Melissa asks students to engage in a think-pair-share activity to respond to this question: "How has your thinking about Brain changed over time?"

Key Strategies to Help You Teach Comprehension

In the following pages of this chapter, I have gathered both new and familiar instructional strategies and practices from teachers, researchers, and my own experience. You can use these five strategies to build students' comprehension skills but also to build capacity in the other components of reading—decoding, fluency, and vocabulary—all of which will help students travel further along the pathway to comprehension.

1. Engage students in self-aware, active reading
2. Teach the practices of good readers
3. Teach text structures
4. Seek out mentor texts
5. Organize book clubs

1. Engage Students in Self-Aware, Active Reading

Reading has its ups and downs. Sometimes it's easy and sometimes it's hard. You can empower students to take action when it's hard—give them the can-do attitude that will get them through the hard bits.

This strategy is simple: talk to your students about both your experience as a reader and their experiences as readers. Help them become self-aware of reading as a *process they experience*. If asked, students will happily tell you about times when reading is fun and accomplished with ease. For instance, when you project a Calvin and Hobbs cartoon for students to read and respond to. Or when you give them time to choose a book to read for a set period of time during the day.

Students will also recognize what you mean when you say that sometimes reading is a grind, when the concepts are complex, the vocabulary is unfamiliar, or the text requires background knowledge that they don't have. These all stand in the way of comprehension.

When reading is a grind, students begin to doubt themselves and give up. You can help them realize that *you*, their teacher, sometimes finds reading hard too. This knowledge can be very reassuring. If you can find a way to talk about your reading challenges with students, they will follow your lead. They won't try to hide the difficulties they experience.

One way to encourage this mindset is through a mini-lesson on active reading, as demonstrated by teacher Lisa.

Teaching Tip

If you can find a way to talk about your reading challenges with students, they will follow your lead. They won't try to hide the difficulties they experience.

In Lisa's Classroom: Hurdle Jumping

Grade 3 teacher Lisa uses a brilliant analogy to help her students understand active reading. She begins by telling her students that good readers are active readers. She says that readers sometimes don't understand what they are reading or get bored or get stuck. And then she tells them this is *normal*. That's important.

Lisa wants to make sure that her students do not lose their self-confidence when they face challenges. She has seen it happen far too often.

Lisa assures her students, "All readers get stuck sometimes and when that happens, they have to be active readers and do something!" She tells her students that she is going to teach them a strategy that will help them be active readers. "Being an active reader," she says, "means knowing that you have to do something when you get stuck or when reading gets hard."

Lisa shows an image of an athlete running down a track toward a hurdle and says, "Do you see how the person is running down the track? That is like you when you are reading. You are actively involved in your reading. Right now, just like the runner, everything is going smoothly. There is nothing in your way that makes reading hard. You understand what you are reading—you might be learning something new, or you might be enjoying a favorite book."

Lisa points. "But look ahead. What do you see?"

The students tell her they see something in the way, on the track. One student volunteers, "It's a hurdle. My sister runs track, and she jumps them."

Lisa says, "That's right! It is a hurdle, and the runner must jump over the hurdle to keep going. That's just like reading."

Lisa pauses for effect. "Once in a while, when you read, you come to a word that you don't know. It's like a hurdle has been placed in front of you. Has that ever happened to you?"

Several students raise their hands. Lisa continues, "It happens to me sometimes, too. That's normal for readers. When my reading gets hard, though, I know there are some things I can do to help myself."

Lisa asks her students to think of a time when reading was hard for them and what they did to jump those hurdles. She uses a T-chart to record their answers. On one side, she records a time they remember when reading was hard and on the other side, she writes down what they did about it.

Next, Lisa shows her students an anchor chart (see below) she has created on poster paper with a list of strategies she uses when she has a reading hurdle to get over. After she reads these aloud to her students, Lisa pulls out the book, *Junkyard Wonders* by Patricia Polacco, a wonderful book about a young girl who has trouble learning to read. The book is full of rich vocabulary.

Lisa reads the book, demonstrating what she does to be an active reader. She pauses on each page. When she pauses, she shows her students what she looks like as she uses each of the strategies on the chart.

At the end of the lesson, Lisa tells her students that they can refer to the anchor chart when they are reading and use it to help them practice being active readers.

How to Be an Active Reader

👍 / 👎   I ask myself questions like, "What does this remind me of?"

👍 / 👎   I stop reading for a minute or slow down to see if I can remember what I read.

👍 / 👎   I go back and look at pictures or diagrams.

👍 / 👎   I reread sections that I have already read.

👍 / 👎   I try to picture what I am reading by closing my eyes and visualizing what is happening.

👍 / 👎   I write things down like the names of the characters or the parts of a plant.

👍 / 👎   I say to myself, "Could I tell someone else what this is about?"

Creating Self-Aware, Active Readers

Have you heard the phrase, "children are natural born thinkers"? Children have the drive and ability to wonder about everything under the sun. You can harness that curiosity. Even the youngest students can learn to be constantly self-aware about how they read. Walk your students through the following steps to help them learn how being self-aware as readers, they can take action to help themselves.

Choose a text to read aloud to your students that will allow students to use four active reading strategies. For intermediate students, I would suggest the book *Owl Moon* by Jane Yolen to teach students how to use visualization and ask questions as they read.

Spark the metacognition mindset. Tell the story of the hurdle jumper from the feature "In Lisa's Classroom" on pages 134–135.

Introduce the activity. Recreate the four-quadrant graphic organizer (on the next page) on a piece of chart paper in front of your students. Choose four "active reader" strategies to introduce to your students or use the four listed here.

- Picture it.
- Ask questions.
- Slow down and go back.
- Write it down.

Tell your students you are going to read the book aloud. Ask them to help you use the graphic organizer with the strategies to be active readers.

Picture it. If you are using *Owl Moon*, read the following lines aloud without showing students the book's illustrations:

> It was late one winter night, long past my bedtime, when Papa and I went owling. There was no wind. The trees stood still as giant statues. And the moon was so bright the sky seemed to shine.

Next, point to the graphic organizer and encourage students to think while they read.

- Say, for instance, "I want to picture what I am reading right now. Can you help me? What are you picturing?" Some students will say they picture a dark night, others will say they see tall trees, and still others will say they see the countryside.
- You say, "I am going to put a check mark in the box on the graphic organizer that says 'Picture it' because that is what we just did to help us be active readers."
- Tell students that they can draw the pictures they see in their minds, later. Invite a student to come up to the chart and draw a picture in response to the text.

Ask questions. Choose the words you want to teach to your students.

- Say, "There is something I read that I don't understand. It was the word *owling*. I wonder what *owling* means?"
- Tell students, "I just asked myself a question, which is being an active reader." Point to the graphic organizer where it says, "Ask questions" and write the question there.

Children have the drive and ability to wonder about everything under the sun. You can harness that curiosity!

I Can Be an Active Reader

Student name: _____

Ask questions.	Slow down and go back.
Picture it.	Write it down.

Pembroke Publishers ©2021 *Sometimes Reading Is Hard* by Robin Bright ISBN 978-1-55138-351-4

- Then ask students what they think the word *owling* means. Record their ideas. For example, "It might mean they find owls." Or "It's hunting."

Slow down and go back. Read several pages aloud. When you come to the line, "When you go owling you have to be brave," stop and say, "I think I remember that there was something else you have to do when you go owling." Ask those who remember (and hopefully some students will remember) not to tell you the answer because you want to figure it out for yourself. "I am going to go back and reread a little bit so I can figure it out myself!" Flip back several pages. Show students you found the page and read the line, "If you go owling, you have to be quiet, that's what Pa always says." Say, "It helped me to go back to reread. It's a good strategy!"

If you want to discuss this further, you might ask, "Why do you think you have to be those two things when you go owling?"

Write it down. Jot down something that you learn from the story. For example, you might tell students that you want to remember the two things that you have to do when you go owling—to be quiet and to be brave—and so you are going to write these on the graphic organizer. Say, "Writing down is another good strategy to help me remember things as I read!"

Offer encouragement. After using a few strategies, you might say something like, "Look at us. We are being active readers and you are helping me understand what I am reading." Continue to read. Pause and use the graphic organizer when there are opportunities to practice the four ways to be active, self-aware readers.

Practice. Give students a copy of their own graphic organizers. They can practice the active reader strategies alone or with a partner when reading another text.

Reflect. At the end of the session, meet with your students all together, perhaps in the meeting area of the classroom, to reflect on the active reader strategies they have been introduced to and practiced. You might suggest that they use the graphic organizer any time they read, to help them get over the hurdles.

· ·

2. Teach the Practices of Good Readers

Self-aware, active readers are good readers. They use "good reader" practices, or habits, to help them comprehend what they read. Good readers use the practices, sometimes without even realizing they are doing so.

I have found as many as 12 "good reader" practices (sometimes called strategies) in the research literature. In my judgement, the following six are all the practices students need to help them develop their comprehension skills.

Students need to know why you want them to learn these practices, that is, to enhance comprehension. The six practices I recommend you encourage students to learn and use to improve their reading comprehension are predicting, questioning, connecting, visualizing, summarizing, and inferring.

What Do Good Readers Do When They Read?

Good readers make predictions before and during reading.
What do good readers do? They think and wonder about the text as they read. Their own thoughts and ideas combine with what they see in the text, so that they can make predictions about the text. They continue to read to confirm or change their predictions.

The six essential practices of a good reader:
- makes predictions
- asks questions
- makes connections
- visualizes
- summarizes
- makes inferences

How can I support prediction in my teaching? Encourage prediction by making it a habit to predict before you read any text aloud. When reading from a book, have students examine the cover illustration and title. Discuss the author and illustrator. Ask students what they think the book will be about.

If you use a textbook with older students, ask them to look at the cover, the table of contents, and information about the author. Ask them what they think the text will be about. You may even want them to scan a chapter so that they can make predictions based on what they gather from headings and visuals. For all students, use prediction throughout reading by stopping at key points and asking them if previous predictions were confirmed or not, and what they think will be coming next.

Good readers ask questions while they read.

Helping students pose questions helps them articulate and ruminate about their expectations.

What do good readers do? They ask questions that they are naturally curious about before and during reading. Readers generally have expectations about the texts before and while reading. Helping students pose questions helps them articulate and ruminate about their expectations. Questions might centre around the meaning of a word or phrase. "What does _____ mean?"

How can I support questioning in my teaching? Model asking questions that you as a reader genuinely have about the text. For instance, you might ask, "Why did Chrysanthemum's feelings about her name change after she started school?" while reading that wonderful book of the same name by Kevin Henkes. With older students, you might ask, "What do you know about the author of this piece? What might have motivated the author to write this? Do we suspect a bias in the writing?"

Good readers make connections as they read.

What do good readers do? They say to themselves, "This reminds me of_____" as they read. They connect what they are reading with their own lives, with other texts they have read, and with what they know about the world. Research shows that when readers make different kinds of connections with text, they remember and comprehend better.

How can I support making connections in my teaching? Help support students to make three kinds of connections: text to self, text to text, and text to world. Encourage the use of stems like these:

- I can relate to_____ because _____.
- I have read something else like this.
- This is similar to/different from_____.
- That part reminds me of ______ in the real world.

Good readers visualize what they read.

What do good readers do? They picture what they are reading about. They might picture the place, a character, or an action. Visualizing as you read helps support comprehension. It also helps you remember what you have read.

How can I support visualizing in my teaching? Tell students that you want them to "make a picture" in their minds while reading—some teachers call this "making a movie" in your head. Descriptive texts lend themselves to practicing this strategy. You can invite students to draw or sketch during a reading, adding words or phrases to help them understand what they read. If you read aloud to students, have them tell you if the main character reminds them of someone and to picture that person as you continue to read.

My "Good Reader" Practices

PREDICT	QUESTION
I predict …	My questions are …

CONNECT	VISUALIZE
This reminds me of …	I can picture …

SUMMARIZE	INFER
This is about …	I can tell … because …

Pembroke Publishers ©2021 *Sometimes Reading Is Hard* by Robin Bright ISBN 978-1-55138-351-4

Good readers summarize what they have read.

What do good readers do? They think about what they have read and are able to retell the main idea and supporting details to others orally or in a written form. Knowing how to summarize a text helps students remember what they read.

How can I support summarizing in my teaching? Explain summarizing, which is to explain the main idea of what you read. Tell students that summarizing helps them to remember and learn from reading. You might ask students to use the turn-and-talk strategy at various junctures during paired reading. During a pause, one student explains to their partner what they have read. Then the second student paraphrases what the first student said and adds any additional information. Students can use the "who, what, when, and where" approach to summarize their reading. You can also have students retell stories and create story maps, so that they use their own words to show their understanding of what they have read.

Good readers make inferences as they read.

What do good readers do? They draw conclusions about the text based not on what was communicated explicitly in print, but based on clues from the text. You may know this strategy as "reading between the lines." Readers often unconsciously use clues in the text to help them make sense of what is happening.

How can I support making inferences in my teaching? Read a short paragraph to students and then have them tell you everything they know based on what you read. Draw two columns on the board. Record what students tell you was clearly stated in one column and record what they inferred from the text in the second column. Talk about how much readers learn from a text that isn't actually stated in the text.

Even very young students know how to infer. For example, after I had read aloud Robert Munsch's book *Love You Forever* to a Grade 1 class, a student piped up and said, "Awww, the son is very sad." Nowhere in the book do those words appear. The illustrations do not even show the son's face. The student had made an inference. Asking students how they arrive at certain understandings and conclusions help them and other students learn how to infer intentionally. The stem "I know _____ because_____" is very helpful when you want students to tell you how they make certain inferences.

The Power of the Think-Aloud

You are already aware that the read-aloud works beautifully for teaching vocabulary (Chapter 4, pages 104–107). During a read-aloud, you pause for conversation and teach while you are reading using a turn and talk approach with students. In a think-aloud, you *model your thinking* as you read. I love the description that a think-aloud is "eavesdropping on someone's thinking." You can use a think-aloud that includes modelling and guided practice to teach six essential reading practices that lead to comprehension.

- A think-aloud is the process of verbalizing the thinking that happens while engaging in a skill. We can use it to verbalize our thoughts as we model a good reading practice.
- Modelling is the demonstration of a skill. We can use it to demonstrate the practice of a good reader.
- Guided practice is when students practice the skill with assistance from others.

Teaching Tip

Students who are still learning to decode might not be able to use any of the comprehension practices while reading, as they are still working on "translating" the letters into words. What those students need is explicit, targeted instruction on the pathway skills of decoding, fluency, and vocabulary. You can still teach comprehension practices, though, through oral discussions of shared text.

In her book *Interactive Think-Aloud Lessons: 25 Surefire Ways to Engage Students and Improve Comprehension*, Lori Oczkus (2009) describes the necessary steps to teach comprehension practices. This is Lori's version of the "I Do, We Do, You Do it Together, You Do it Alone" teaching strategy also known as the "Gradual Release of Responsibility Model (GRR)" (Pearson & Gallagher, 1983). Following this model, students see a practice modelled and try it out before they use it on their own. Lori's think-aloud protocol suggests that you use the first five steps outlined below. I have added a sixth step so that you can observe how individual students demonstrate using the comprehension practices.

Protocol for Teaching Good Reading Practices through a Think-Aloud

Use a short text such as a picture book that will interest all students.

1. **Introduce the practice** in a fun and easy-going manner. The main thing is to name it.
2. **Define or explain the practice** in a student-friendly, clear, and explicit way that tells students the purpose for using it while reading.
3. **Model using the practice** using the text, additional props, and chart paper. This is where you think out loud in front of your students. Elementary students will appreciate and remember the practices best when you dress up like a character or bring in a prop that represents the practice.
4. **Provide guidance while students use the practice in pairs** so that students can try it out with a text while working collaboratively to support one another's learning. Maintain your involvement in the process, asking questions and providing prompts, gradually turning over the responsibility of students' use of the practice to them.
5. **Reflect on the practice** by having students gather in a circle to talk about how they used the strategy and any problems that came up.
6. **Provide independent practice** after students have had several opportunities to use it.

STEP BY STEP: Good Readers Do This

Let's see how to use the think-aloud protocol to teach a group of Grade 4 students one of the six practices of good readers, for the purposes of boosting comprehension. (When I created the following lesson, I was inspired by the work of Lori Oczkus (2009) and P. David Pearson & Margaret Gallagher (1983).)

Introduce the practice. Begin by saying, "Today, I am going to teach you a strategy that good readers use when they read. This practice is called "making predictions." For elementary and middle school students, author Lori Oczkus suggests that teachers use a character, a hand gesture, and an artifact to introduce the strategy. For example, for predicting, Lori suggests the character could be Peter the Powerful Predictor, the hand gesture could be a hand moving over a crystal ball, and the artifact could be a glass ball (a snow globe or ornament). You can use your imagination to come up with a character, gesture, and artifact that fit your own classroom context.

Define or explain the practice. Next, say, "Before reading, a powerful predictor examines the book and makes predictions or educated guesses about what

Teaching Tip

You can apply this step-by-step method to teach any one of the six practices of good readers. To review, they are
- make predictions
- ask questions
- make connections
- visualize
- summarize
- make inferences

the book will be about. During reading, a powerful predictor stops at certain points, and at the end of a page or chapter, and predicts or guesses what will come next." You might add, "Reading isn't just reading the words. Good readers stop and think about what they're reading. They make predictions." Tell the students that making predictions helps you figure out what's going on in the book.

Model the practice with a text. Use a mentor text (a book that lends itself to teaching a particular practice), such as the book *Fireflies* by Julie Brinkloe. Show students the cover and read the title aloud. Ask the students to watch and listen to you as you think out loud to show what making predictions looks like when you read. Say, "I am looking closely at the front cover, and I notice that five people are running and jumping. It looks like they are outside and that it could be nighttime. They are trying to catch yellow lights. I predict that those yellow lights are fireflies because that is the title of the book."

Feel free to involve your students in the think-aloud, too, but keep the focus on what you do as a reader. You can also ask students to tell you what predictions they have about the book, based on what they see on the cover. Ask them to provide reasons for their predictions and respond positively to their ideas, thereby reinforcing their use of the strategy. Conclude by saying, "That's what good readers do—they make predictions just like you did!"

Open the book and after reading the first page say, "Some of our predictions were correct. Did you notice that the author said it was nighttime? The author also wrote that the yellow lights were fireflies." You might want to say that readers do not always get predictions right. Predictions are like estimates; perfection is not required or expected. Continue, "Making predictions helped me read and understand the first page, because I was expecting to read about nighttime and fireflies. When those words were in the story, I could read and understand them easily because of my predictions."

Provide guidance while students use the practice in pairs. Ask students to work together with a partner or in small groups to practice. You might consider using a document projector to continue with the reading of *Fireflies* with your students. Read each page aloud, and then, before turning the page, ask partners to talk to each other and make predictions about what might happen next and why. This encourages students to look for clues in the book to support their predictions. After a few minutes, ask students to share their predictions with you and the class. This step provides important practice for those students who benefit by collaborating and learning from both their teacher and their peers.

Reflect on the use of the practice. At the end of the session, invite students to share what they have learned about the practice and about doing what good readers do. Write these sentence frames on the whiteboard or on chart paper:

- "The practice of _____ helped me because _____."
- "The steps for this practice are _____."
- "I will use the practice _____ again when I _____."

If you notice that students do not seem to get the hang of using the practice, go back and provide more modelling and guided practice.

Provide independent practice. When students are reading independently, observe them as they read. Pause by their desks and ask when they have used the practice of predicting in their own reading. You might give a few examples, offering your own predictions by looking at the covers of books that student has read. They will have no problem correcting you if you get it wrong!

Reteach or remind students of the practices of good readers throughout the year, every year. Eventually, novice readers will pick up on the habits of expert readers.

. . . .

3. Teach Text Structures

Of particular value for comprehending non-fiction is an awareness of text structures.

Text structure can be the actual physical layout of the text. A story and a recipe look quite different on the page. Text structure can also be in the content: how information is communicated, perhaps through a problem in a story that needs to be solved or through a sequence of steps that need to be followed. A story might have an opening, a buildup to a climax, and then a conclusion. A recipe might have a list of ingredients, and then a series of instructions.

> Text structure is like the map of a mall you've never been in before. You can always walk around the mall and figure out where everything is. But if you study the layout of the mall on a map for even a few minutes, you'll navigate through it a lot more effectively.
>
> Similarly, you can read a book without knowing the text structure. But knowing it can help you to understand it better.

Text structures and comprehension go hand in hand by providing clues to students about what to notice when reading a particular text. Students who receive instruction on how a text is organized and structured remember the big ideas and details of what they have read better than those who do not receive such instruction. Recognizing the text structure—such as compare and contrast—while reading contributes to better comprehension outcomes. These findings are observed in a wide range of students from Kindergarten to high school as well as for English language learners and students who appear to struggle with reading. It makes teaching text structures an obvious choice.

For fiction texts such as short stories, picture books, and novels, discussing genre (types of books) will aid comprehension. Help students identify what makes a text historical fiction, fantasy, or a fairytale. You will recognize the most common text structure in fiction: beginning (the set up), middle (problem), and ending (climax and resolution). This structure is often communicated through what we call story elements, which may include setting, characters, problem, action, and resolution.

The five main text structures that are taught through non-fiction mentor texts:
- description
- sequence
- compare and contrast *~ Grandma & Gogg*
- problem and solution
- cause and effect

By grasping what text structures are being used, the student has a better chance of understanding what they read. For example, a student will get a lot more out of a text about bicycle repair if they can recognize that a series of numbered sentences is actually a set of sequenced instructions.

Readers get better at using good reader comprehension strategies like making predictions ("I know what is coming next"), connecting ("I see how those two ideas are related, one is a cause and one is an effect"), and summarizing ("I can tell someone the main ideas of what I have read") when they are familiar with text structures.

4. Seek Out Mentor Texts

Mentor texts are those beloved, well-worn, dog-eared picture books, poems, and newspaper clippings that you return to again and again to teach a particular concept, practice, skill, or strategy. I have my favorites, like *Fireflies* by Julie Brinkloe, and I am sure you have yours.

A Mentor Text for Younger Students

The use of mentor texts is really all about learning from the best, isn't it?

The use of mentor texts is really all about learning from the best, isn't it? One of my favorites is *The Important Book* by Margaret Wise Brown. Over the years, I have used this special book with elementary, middle school, undergraduate, and graduate students. I use it along with the think-aloud protocol, to find compelling main ideas in a text, a skill that is crucial for comprehension.

In this timeless book, the author writes,

> The important thing about rain is
> that it is wet.

The author goes on to describe rain in multiple ways. Finally, though, she circles back to repeat the first line. Students understand almost immediately how this text calls attention to the main idea that rain is wet. This makes it ideal for teaching about main ideas. Mentor texts are valuable when teaching all of the six good-reader comprehension practices.

A Mentor Text for Older Students

Some mentor texts are simply excerpts from books that you find compelling and want to share with your students again and again. One mentor text I use is *Things They Carried* by Tim O'Brien. I read an excerpt from this gripping, heart-wrenching book about war to older students, both for its content and to build background knowledge. After students read about what the soldiers brought along with them on their missions to Vietnam, both literally (M-16 rifles and foot powder) and figuratively (grief and terror), students connect with the text by thinking about what they carry in their own lives. This has sparked many an interesting discussion about how to read metafiction, autofiction, and autobiography. And it helps students read and understand a text about war when they have not experienced it.

What to Look for in Mentor Texts

To teach prediction. Check out books that contain a sense of what might happen next on each page, like cliffhangers. Seek books that students seemingly cannot put down and that have a satisfying resolution.

To teach questioning. Check out books that contain some ambiguity and uncertainty. Seek books that make the reader wonder.

To teach connecting. Check out books that will remind students of their own lives, of their experiences, and of the world they know. Seek books about feelings and emotions that students experience, such as frustration, worry, nervousness, excitement, and embarrassment.

To teach visualizing. Check out fiction and non-fiction books and poetry that help readers make mental images while reading. Seek books with descriptive or figurative language.

To teach summarizing. Check out books that have an obvious sequential plot: this happens, then this, and then that. Seek non-fiction books that contain lots of interesting information that students can connect with and share.

To teach inferring. Check out books that contain information that both drives the plot and is descriptive. Seek books that the reader can make sense of only by combining what the text says with what they know.

5. Organize Book Clubs

Oprah Winfrey says that the reward of joining a book club is being able to expand your mind and have new experiences and ideas. Isn't that exactly what we want reading to do for our students?

Are you part of a book club? This popular phenomenon owes something of its origin to the influential Oprah Winfrey. The author, producer, and talk show host began her Oprah's Book Club in 1996. Oprah says that she began her televised book club for the same reasons that many of us join our own book clubs: to read books and talk about them with others.

Book clubs, sometimes referred to as literature circles, is a strategy that places students in small groups to read and discuss a book (or a chapter of a book) that they have read on their own. Ideally, you would provide students with several highly engaging texts for each club to choose from. The purpose of book clubs, according to literacy experts, is to deepen students' understanding of a common text. In other words, they are perfect for building comprehension skills.

You may wish to monitor student discussion to ensure that readers work at developing a deeper understanding of the text by interacting with others.

In Marlin's Classroom: Book Clubs for Comprehension

Marlin, a recently retired teacher with 30 years of teaching experience, tells me that he has "always been inspired to seek out strategies that motivate my students to become better readers, while helping them understand and care about what they read." He employs the framework of the stages of the reading process, using the phrases, "into the text" "through the text," and "beyond the text" to develop comprehension.

For book clubs, Marlin uses the kit called *Ready, Set, Adventure!* from Moving Up with Literacy Place (Scholastic Canada). It includes books on the theme of adventure, and sets of questions on three spinners for use before, during, and after reading. The idea is that students can use these questions to prompt discussion in their groups.

Before students begin, however, Marlin does a comprehensive read-aloud with students to demonstrate how to discuss a text together to build comprehension. He sparks students' interest by telling them that they will get to read their own adventure stories in a book club.

The read-aloud consists of four sections:

- **To begin**. Marlin draws on students' prior knowledge on the theme of adventure and records it in a concept web. This helps build vocabulary based on the theme of adventure.
- **Into the text**. Marlin previews the book with students, looking for clues on the front and back covers and discussing predicting questions.
- **Through the text**. While Marlin reads the text, he stops periodically to discuss questions with students or to define difficult vocabulary. After the reading is finished, they discuss what makes the story an adventure story. They add ideas to the concept web they had begun earlier.
- **Beyond the text**. After the reading, Marlin posts a piece of chart paper in front of the class and distributes large sticky notes. He asks students to write their responses to various questions about the text. And then they talk about their responses as a whole class.

After the read-aloud, Marlin organizes students into their book club groups based on what he knows about their reading proficiency. He provides each group with individual copies of their book, along with three comprehension spinners for before, during, and after their reading. (You could simply make your own lists of questions for students, but the spinners are more fun.)

Marlin assigns students with book club jobs: a comprehension coordinator, a noise controller, an encourager, and a spinner/timekeeper.

This is how Marlin reflects on this strategy:

This strategy is fresh and innovative. It is exciting for the students to collaborate while developing their comprehension skills. Students learn to think about and practice what they do as readers when they move into, through, and beyond the text. The book clubs offer opportunities for small-group reading while deepening comprehension. It provides student control and independence in the reading process.

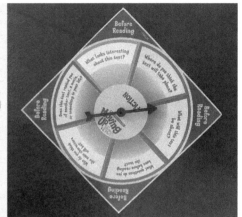

Your Key Takeaways

Here are the key ideas we explored in this chapter on teaching comprehension.

- Comprehension is the process of constructing meaning from texts. The thrill of comprehension depends on the successful development of decoding, fluency, and vocabulary skills.
- Comprehension is an interactive process that combines what goes on in the text with what goes on in the head.
- Students' motivation and confidence affect comprehension.
- The stages of the reading process assist you in developing students' comprehension.
- Students use the practices of good readers to improve their comprehension, and thereby make their reading more enjoyable and meaningful.
- You can use the gradual release of responsibility model to teach the practices of good readers.
- Teaching text structures enhances comprehension for all students.
- When students meet in books clubs to discuss what they have read, they deepen their understanding and learn to appreciate multiple perspectives.

6

Sustaining the Journey: How to Inspire Your Students to Love Reading

---

For students of every ability and background, it's the simple, miraculous act of reading a good book that turns them into readers, because even for the least experienced, most reluctant reader, it's the one good book that changes everything. The job of adults who care about reading is to move heaven and earth to put that book into a child's hands.
—Nancie Atwell (2007)

Knowing how to read and how to teach reading are at once exhilarating, complex, challenging, and rewarding experiences. It is my hope that the preceding chapters have helped refresh your appreciation for what is involved in the extraordinary act of learning how to read and the honorable effort to teach reading.

Knowing *how* to read should not be the end of the road for our students, however. Reading can and should be a lifelong pleasure. Unfortunately, many students and adults are what we call "aliterate"—they choose not to read despite knowing how to read. Aliteracy is a problem with many students who do not perceive reading to be either valuable or interesting, especially in comparison with activities that they do enjoy. Over time, as reading becomes less and less frequent, it becomes less and less attractive. Getting these individuals back into reading may seem an insurmountable task.

The One Book That Changes Everything!

As teachers of reading, our job is to help students find the one book that changes everything.

When a reader finds that one book that they love, it's a wonderful feeling. This moment can be the one that kick-starts reading for that student, beginning a journey down the path of lifelong reading. I strongly believe that, as teachers of reading, our job is to help students find *the one book that changes everything*. That book may or may not be on a bestsellers' list. All it needs to do is appeal to that one reader in your class who needs it. In response to the annual unveiling of "best" and "favorite" booklists, Kari, a parent and bookseller, tweeted the following:

You know what the best book of the year was? … The one that a striving reader stuck with until the very end. The one that made a child ask for a sequel. The one that a child saw themselves in. If a book was loved by one, it's the best book! (Tanaka, 2020)

I couldn't agree more! Finding the one right book is often all that stands in the way of showing students they can love reading. A student's love for a single book can be powerful not only for developing components of reading but for motivating students to want to read and to keep reading. My own two daughters remember the special books that they loved growing up and maybe you do too. You might recognize some of their favorites: *Chasing Redbird* by Sharon Creech, The Roman Mysteries book series by Caroline Lawrence, *The Golden Compass* by Philip Pullman, and *The King in the Window* by Adam Gopnik to name a few. These books transformed my daughters into passionate readers because they lost themselves in the stories.

That transformation only happens when skilled readers find the right books. The reader starts with a few words and then a few sentences, and then, if all goes well, they never look back. Have you ever finished a book and known you simply *had* to find other books by the same author? Or find other books in the same genre? Here is what a group of six- and seven-year-olds say about reading.

- "I like reading to my baby brother."
- "I like to read by myself and I like reading with my friends."
- "Reading is my favorite thing."
- "I get a good feeling when I read."
- "Some books are really funny, so I read them over and over again."

These young students have good feelings about reading. Once they have that, all you have to do is keep them on the path.

In Kristen's Classroom: It Was My Favorite Book When I Was Your Age

Kristen, a Grade 6 teacher, tells of her experience sharing with her students a book that was close to her heart:

I remember being transformed as a reader by the story and book by Anne Frank: *The Diary of a Young Girl*. The story is well-known to most adults, but seldom have my Grade 6 students heard of it when I first introduce it to them. It is an amazing true story of a young girl's experience of World War II. Anne, along with her family, hides to avoid capture during the German occupation of Holland. I always share this book as a novel study with my students.

At first, I would say about half of my students look forward to our reading of this book, especially when I say it is about World War II and that it is written by a young girl in diary form. Others less aware of the circumstances around World War II take a bit longer to get into the book, but they always do. It's like the book itself casts a spell over them, and they can't wait for me to read it to them each day. My students find they relate to Anne's experiences with her teacher, playing with Peter's cat, and writing poetry to give as gifts.

Following our reading of the story, my students choose arts-based projects to do in response to the book. We share their work in a one-hour "Ceremony of Learning," during which we transform our classroom into a theatre and share reports, poetry, narration, drama, and music to remember Anne.

I would say that my students' interest in reading about a young girl during World War II is not great before we start reading the book together, but that changes quickly. My students cannot help but be interested and captivated by this story.

Key Strategies for Inspiring a Life-Long Relationship with Reading

In the pages that follow in this chapter, I have gathered both new and familiar instructional practices and strategies gathered from teachers, researchers, and my own experience. You can use these five strategies to help your students develop a personal connection with reading that transforms reading from a chore to a delight and a passion. The practices below depend on the development of the four components of reading—decoding, fluency, vocabulary, and comprehension—and help students cement a lifelong positive relationship with reading.

1. Bring picture books into students' lives
2. Provide diverse literature
3. Use reading interest surveys
4. Visit libraries with your students
5. Create a classroom library

1. Bring Picture Books into Students' Lives

Picture books might be the key to inspiring your students as readers. Grade 2 teacher Michelle begins almost every day with a picture book because, she says, they draw students into a topic and get them interested in what they are learning. Michelle can find a picture book for every topic in a curriculum and for situations that come up spontaneously in class.

The importance of the simple act of finding books that peak students' interest cannot be overstated. Picture books belong in every classroom at every grade level, even in high school. There, I've said it. The combination of the visual and literary arts wins hearts. Picture books represent and celebrate diversity. They offer a variety of perspectives. They offer a "way in" to difficult subjects. They are accessible for almost all readers. And many of them do all this in 32 pages. They are likely the best mentor texts you can use.

I can think of no better way to inspire reading than through the well-chosen picture book. Good films, like today's picture books, operate on more than one level. For example, Pixar's *Inside Out*, while being a delightful story of a child struggling to handle her family's move to a new city, is also a remarkable portrayal of the science behind the brain, memory, sleep, and emotion.

Picture books often do the same thing. Think of Sydney Smith's book *Small in the City*. On the surface, the book is narrated by a child in a city, first riding a bus and then walking home as a winter storm takes hold. The child seems to be telling the reader about the neighborhood. But then the reader figures out that the child is talking about something else entirely. That's when emotions, feelings, and memories take over. Readers are immersed in seeing through another's eyes.

Picture books belong in every classroom at every grade level, even in high school. There, I've said it.

You can play a role in regularizing the reading of picture books—and graphic novels as well—throughout the grades by having them in your classroom, reading aloud from them, using them in teaching, and offering them to students for leisure reading. By making your use of picture books normal, even your more accomplished readers will not hesitate to reach for them.

Today, picture books and graphic novels are sensitively written, brilliantly illustrated, and marketed for all ages. They explore diverse and big idea topics in areas such as perseverance, happiness, anxiety, the environment, peace, war, emotions and regulation of emotions, diversity, ideation, life and death, empathy, generosity, disability, and ADHD, just for starters. These books are informational, comforting, and allow readers to "pass over" into the experiences of others, paving the way for empathy and understanding. This makes them especially important in middle and high school classrooms as well as elementary classrooms.

Amazing Picture Books for all Classrooms

For children in elementary grades:

Fitting in
- *Yeti and the Bird* by Nadia Shireen
- *I Talk Like a River* by Jordan Scott
- *Your Name Is a Song* by Jamilah Thompkins-Bigelow

Inner courage
- *Sulwe* by Lupita Nyong'o
- *When You Are Brave* by Pat Zietlow Miller
- *I Can Do Hard Things* by Gabi Garcia

Hobbies
- *Insects Are My Life* by Megan McDonald
- *Hannah's Collections* by Marthe Jocelyn
- *Count on Me* by Miguel Tanco

Kindness
- *The Power of One* by Trudy Ludwig
- *Just Ask* by Sonia Sotomayor
- *The Day You Begin* by Jacqueline Woodson

Social-emotional well-being
- *Happy Right Now* by Julie Berry
- *The Cool Bean* by Jory John
- *I Am One* by Susan Verde

For older students:

Environmental issues
- *Gone Is Gone* by Isabelle Groc
- *One Earth: People of Color Protecting Our Planet* by Anuradha Rao
- *Not Your Typical Book about the Environment* by Elin Kelsey

Immigration
- *The Arrival* by Shaun Tan
- *Count Me In* by Varsha Bajaj
- *Dreamers* by Yuyi Morales

Social-emotional well-being
- *B Is for Breathe: The ABCs of Coping with Fussy and Frustrating Feelings* by Dr. Melissa Munro Boyd
- *Goodnight iPad* by Ann Droyd
- *The Book of Mistakes* by Corinna Luyken

Residential schools
- *I Am Not a Number* by Jenny Kay Dupuis and Kathy Kacer
- *Secret Path* by Gord Downie and Jeff Lemire
- *The Orange Shirt Story* by Phyllis Webstad

Courage
- *Malala's Magic Pencil* by Malala Yousafzai
- *Emmanuel's Dream* by Laurie Ann Thompson
- *Say Something!* by Peter H. Reynolds

Homelessness
- *I See You* by Michael Genhart
- *Changing Places: A Kids' View of Shelter Living* by Margie Chalofsky, Glen Finland, and Judy Wallace
- *A Shelter in Our Car* by Monica Gunning

A book I have relied on to find great book titles for kids, teachers, and parents alike is *The Story Cure: An A-Z of Books to Keep Kids Happy, Healthy and Wise*. Bibliotherapists Ella Berthoud and Susan Elderkin provide hundreds of book ideas on topics ranging from "moving and leaving friends behind" to "having to practice a musical instrument" and from "wanting to own a pet" to "feeling like an outsider." A resource like this belongs on your bookshelf.

2. Provide Diverse Literature

Multicultural education scholar Rudine Sims Bishop writes,

> Books are sometimes windows, offering views of worlds that may be real or imagined, familiar or strange. These windows are also sliding glass doors, and readers have only to walk through in imagination to become part of whatever world has been created or recreated by the author. Literature transforms human experience and reflects it back to us, and in that reflection we can see our own lives and experiences as part of a larger human experience. Reading, then, becomes a means of self-affirmation, and readers often seek their mirrors in books.

What's on Your Bookshelf?

Who chooses the books in your classroom? For the most part, you do. I recall asking my pre-service teachers to consider the question, "Who has the greatest influence on choosing which books are used in the classroom?" We had a spirited discussion. Students named curriculum writers, parents, school boards, and others as influential in deciding what books and resources they were allowed to use. When I told them that they missed identifying the teacher as having a huge influence on what books are placed in front of their students, they were horrified to have missed the obvious.

As a teacher, you have a great deal of latitude in selecting the literature and texts you present to your students. And even if some texts are mandatory, you still get to decide how to teach them. What my pre-service teachers overlooked is that teachers are often the most influential gatekeepers—some would say censors—of literature coming into the classroom, even though we often think it is other groups who limit reading choices.

It is the power of this position that gives you a huge responsibility to know the breadth of literature available and to ensure that you can offer students a wide and representative selection. The more you know about diverse books, the better you can meet students' reading interests and encourage reading beyond the classroom.

It is the power of your position that gives you a huge responsibility to know the breadth of literature available and to ensure that you can offer students a wide and representative selection.

Why You Should Include Diverse Literature in Your Classroom

Most classrooms today include students with a wide variety of backgrounds. Religion, culture, ethnicity, sexual orientation, and economic status are just a few of the factors that create diversity in the classroom. If your selection of texts does not include representation of your students and authors with a similar variety of backgrounds, you will have missed a powerful opportunity to inspire readers.

When you help your students see themselves represented in books, you help them realize that they are valued members of society. Students develop self-confidence, a sense of belonging, and validation when books are mirrors that reflect who they are, what they experience, and how they matter.

Students learn that authors are people who were children and youth just like them. They learn that their own experiences and stories may be worthy of being told.

Above and beyond these benefits, don't forget interest. By using a text that reflects a child's reality, you may spark their interest in a book that really means something to them. Once you have them reading, their reading skills will improve, and you thereby launch them along the path to a lifetime of reading.

Students from all walks of life, however, benefit from exposure to diversity through the literature you provide to them.

- Students can recognize and learn about various languages, cultures, and peoples.
- They can learn about others' lives and experiences and thereby see how we are all more alike than different.
- They can develop empathy by learning about the experiences of others.
- They may learn about historical events and individuals in a wide variety of arenas such as art, music, literature, mathematics, and science who may not be included in their education otherwise.
- They may be inspired by the breadth and variety of story that diverse literature provides.

For some students, the classroom is a rare safe place, where they can ask questions and talk about issues, concerns, and fears without fear of judgement, by exploring the experiences of fictional and real characters in books.

Writer, book reviewer, and librarian Ken Setterington says, "Diversity has always been a hallmark of children's literature, with publishers pushing the boundaries of what's accepted." (Miller Oke, 2019) Reading diverse books means self-affirmation for many students. These books also build community unity and inclusivity. Because classrooms are safe communities for students, diverse books open up room for conversations about important but difficult topics, such as homelessness, bullying, refugee experiences, and racism.

Diverse Books for the Classroom

- *Free Lunch* by Rex Ogle (ages 9–12)
- *Stolen Words* by Melanie Florence (ages 5–8)
- *American Born Chinese* by Gene Luen Yang (ages 12+)
- *The Hate U Give* by Angie Thomas (ages 12+)
- *Fish in a Tree* by Lynda Mullaly Hunt (ages 10+)
- *Amina's Voice* by Hena Khan (ages 8–12)
- *I Am Enough* by Grace Byers (ages 4–8)
- *Siha Tooskin Knows the Love of the Dance* by Charlene Bearhead and Wilson Bearhead (ages 9–11)

---

3. Use Reading Interest Surveys

The teacher in me can tell you that when a reader connects with a book, it feels like Katy Perry's inspirational, self-empowerment anthem *Firework* should be playing in the background. The age of the reader makes little difference. Even experienced teachers I work with positively gush over authors and books they didn't know were "out there" until we begin sharing books during my visits to schools.

Finding out what book each student will gush over is one of the most important things that you can do to support interest in reading. Perhaps the most common tool for finding out is the reading interest survey. A well-written survey can open a window on the topics, subjects, issues, and questions that matter to your students. Surveys provide general and specific information about students' reading interests and can be modified to provide oral or written feedback.

The One Thing You Shouldn't Ask: Do You Like Reading?

Older students can fill out reading interest surveys independently, while younger students can do so with either your help or that of caregivers at home. Students' responses to questions about their interests are invaluable in helping you know which books and other reading materials will interest them. You also want to find out how students *feel* about reading. It helps to know what students think are their strengths and challenges as readers. But I should tell you, I see little value in asking a student if they like or don't like reading. It will be obvious. For ideas of what to ask, see the example of a reading interest survey on page 155. You can modify it for the age range of your students and for the kind of information you seek.

Have a good look at the responses you get from students on the reading interest survey. Then ask yourself, How can this new information inform my teaching of reading? If you need ideas for books to match students' interests, ask for advice from your fellow teachers, the school librarian, and booksellers.

Consider sending an email to your students with a personal message with your suggestions. Within the first week of class, I read the students' surveys and send each of them an email with book suggestions based on what they tell me. There is no better way for me to get to know each student, start the relationship on a

Reading Interest Survey

Name: _____

Thank you for taking the time to answer the questions in this short survey. Your responses will help me to get to know you better and to support you over the coming school year.

1. How do you feel about reading? Tell me about it.

_____

2. What types of books do you like to read?

_____

3. List some of your hobbies and things you like to do outside of school.

_____

4. Who are your favorite authors?

_____

5. Tell me a bit about the last book you read that you really enjoyed.

_____

6. Tell me a bit about what you have been doing over the past two months (over the summer). How have you been spending your time?

_____

7. What subjects or topics do you like learning about?

_____

8. If you could read a book about one thing, what would that be?

_____

good footing, and encourage the reading habit at the same time. Here is an email I sent to one of my students linking his interests to potential books he might like.

> Thank you for taking the time to fill out your Reading Interest Survey so thoroughly! I see that, among other things, you like humor and history. I might suggest *Dead End in Norvelt* by Jack Gantos (just about one of the funniest books I have ever read, but YOU will love the historical connections throughout the text.) Jack Gantos has quite an interesting history of his own. He wrote about his early life in the book *A Hole in My Life*, often studied in high school. For something more serious, I'd suggest *Monster* by Walter Dean Myers—a brilliant book touching on the themes of social justice, race, peer pressure, and the justice system. It's a modern classic.

4. Visit Libraries with Your Students

Teaching Tip
One of the best things you can do for students is to help them love the library.

Libraries are the great equalizers of society. They provide free and fantastic access to information and tools that wouldn't otherwise be available to a community. Research from Susan Neumann and David Dickinson (2006) shows that "in middle-income neighborhoods the ratio of books per child is 13 to 1, and in low-income neighborhoods, the ratio is 1 age-appropriate book for every 300 children." Public libraries help make up for that difference. These spaces provide resources for both students and their families.

One of the best things you can do for students is to help them love the library. The school library is the first place to start. It is often the hub of a school, open and inviting to teachers and students throughout the day. But many students do not find their way into the school library except for a weekly classroom visit. High school teachers tell me that most students do not avail themselves of the services in the library *at all*. That is a shame.

To change this situation, visit the school library yourself to learn about the many services and resources a library has to offer and to help students see it as a resource they would like to use. Students who know how to access library support will be more likely to use it to for projects, research, and general interest.

If possible, arrange a visit to the public library in the school neighborhood. Introduce students to a public librarian and let them see what is available to them beyond the school. By exploring the school or public library in a relaxed and fun way, students begin to see the many kinds of reading material available, and hopefully they will be inspired to use it to find books they want to read, both during their school years and long into their adulthood.

Take Your Students on a Scavenger Hunt

Design a scavenger hunt for your students to do while in the library. This can take them a long way in appreciating the many resources available to them not only in school but in the community, too.

You might want to put the information students gather from their scavenger hunt into a google spreadsheet to share with everyone. Consider sending the findings from the library scavenger hunt home in a newsletter in hopes of encouraging families to visit public libraries as well.

Library Scavenger Hunt

Student names: _____

Hello! Today we are going to explore the library so that you can get to know all the amazing books that are here for you. You may conduct the hunt with one or two other students. Please take your time and remember: This is not a race! Libraries are quiet places, so, please, no shouting or running.

Enjoy your time in the school library!

Find a book by an author with a last name that starts with the same letter as your last name.	What book did you find?
Find a book that you have already read.	What book is it? Does this author have other books? If so, please read the blurb on the inside jacket. Is this a book you might want to read? If so, write down its title.
Introduce yourself to the librarian.	What is the librarian's name?
Go to the non-fiction section and find a book that is on a topic that interests you.	Write down the title and one reason you are interested in this topic.
Go to one of the computers in the library and type in the topic you are interested in.	Write down what you find.

Pembroke Publishers ©2021 *Sometimes Reading Is Hard* by Robin Bright ISBN 978-1-55138-351-4

Library Scavenger Hunt cont'd.

Find a book that you want to read and that is a good match for you. Use the five-finger rule to help you make your decision.	What book did you find?
Find a poetry book.	What book did you find?
Find a book with an award sticker on it. Then, go to the library computer and look up the award.	What special recognition did this book receive?
Pick a book from one of the displays.	Write down the title. What is the display about?
Find a book on a topic that you like.	See what you can find out by skimming the pages.
Find a book by the authors Nic Stone and Rebecca Stead.	If you had to choose one of these books to read, which one would it be? Why?
Find a book series on a shelf.	What is the name of the series? Who is the author? How many books are in this series?
Find a book that has great illustrations.	What are the illustrations about?

Pembroke Publishers ©2021 *Sometimes Reading Is Hard* by Robin Bright ISBN 978-1-55138-351-4

5. Create a Classroom Library

We know that reading for pleasure supports comprehension—more access means greater reading gains. It also encourages lifelong learning because it's so easy to get hooked on reading when it's fun. So imagine the service of accessibility you could provide to every single one of your students every day by creating a classroom library full of inviting books.

Teachers curate their own classroom libraries themselves. They often start with just a few books and then build their libraries over time to contain hundreds and even thousands of books. Even with a small classroom library, you can begin to

- share books with students that meet and broaden their reading interests
- show who *you* are as a reader, which serves as an excellent model for your students
- provide reading opportunities for students throughout the school day
- strengthen comprehension by increasing the time students read
- help students learn to choose books that fit their interests and abilities

Teaching Tip

Do not wait for next year or when "the time is right." The time to start building a classroom library is now.

Building a classroom library can be a daunting task that could feel discouraging. But the benefits far outweigh the challenges. The National Council of Teachers of English (NCTE) statement on classroom libraries says that "classroom libraries offer ongoing opportunities for teachers to work with students as individuals to find books that will ignite their love for learning, calm their fears, answer their questions, and improve their lives in any of the multiple ways that only literature can" (2007). So if you haven't started, do not wait for next year or when "the time is right." The time to start building a classroom library is now.

Classroom Library Considerations: For Experts and Beginners

There are many ways to create and maintain a classroom library and have fun doing it. The important thing is to begin. Here are some considerations and resources to help in making a classroom library a vibrant and accessible space.

Your own reading interests matter. What topics or genres interest you? Your own reading interests should be incorporated into the library to ensure that there will be plenty of books in your library that excite you. Any time of day, you should be able to choose a book and talk passionately about it with students.

Seek student volunteers to help. Many students are interested in helping to create libraries in their classrooms. They can be counted on to make signs, provide book synopses, and assist with keeping track of who has what books. Ask for volunteers to help with the task of setting up and maintaining a classroom library.

Start small. Your classroom library does not have to contain hundreds of books to be useful. Be inspired but not intimidated by what others do. Those teachers all had to start somewhere too.

Location, location, location. Students will use the classroom library if it is easily accessible, eye-catching, and comfortable. Set guidelines for its use. For instance, students develop autonomy as readers when they know that they can use the classroom library throughout the day, perhaps when they first arrive, when their other work is done, or during independent reading time.

Variety matters. Provide fiction and non-fiction reading material including a variety of formats, genres, and topics to appeal to a variety of readers.

Include magazines, comic books, and graphic novels. These texts are all fun and engaging. Long, print-heavy books can be intimidating for some students, and they do not suit everyone, especially for leisure reading. Consider including magazines such as

- *National Geographic Kids*: a magazine about the natural world with articles, games, and competitions (for ages 6–14)
- *Chickadee*: a magazine containing stories, games, puzzles, and humor (for ages 6–9)
- *Skipping Stones*: a multicultural global magazine celebrating cultural diversity (for ages 8–16)

Book bins, shelves, and labels. As your classroom library collection develops, consider different ways to organize and display books and other reading materials. You can organize according to genre, format, topic, or theme. Book bins and labels can be helpful.

Care for the materials. Talk to students and display a poster about caring for the classroom library and its contents. Decide on a method for students to sign out the reading material and then return it. In some classrooms, a few volunteers manage the sign-in and sign-out procedures. In other classrooms, students use an honor system to do this themselves.

Teaching Tip: *Subject-Focused Classroom Libraries*

If you are a subject specialist teacher in middle or high school, you can create a subject-focused classroom library for students particularly interested in your area of specialty. I will never forget a story told by Canadian author David Bouchard during a teachers' convention. He recounted that he was not much of a reader in school. He did play sports, however, and he especially admired his high school basketball coach. David said that if his coach had *ever* suggested a book to him, he would have picked it up and read it immediately. Teachers' suggestions carry a lot of power to inspire.

Just Say No to Levelled Libraries

Dr. Alfred Tatum, professor and author, famously wrote, "Levelled text leads to levelled lives" (2017).

The purpose of the classroom library is to develop interest and enjoyment in reading—to *inspire* students to read! Time in the classroom library provides what is sometimes the only opportunity in a school day for students to choose books for reading enjoyment. The classroom library, therefore, is not the place for reading level labels, which box students in to a limited selection of books.

No research study has uncovered evidence that levelled books offer any great reading dividends beyond the primary grades. Irene Fountas and Gay Su Pinnell say as much. They write, "It is our belief that levels have no place in classroom libraries, in school libraries, or on report cards … we certainly never intended that children focus on a label for themselves in choosing books in the classroom libraries." (Parrott, 2017)

In a sense, the classroom library is an extension of school and public libraries, or bookstores. Stock your library with books students will *want* to pick up and read. Then, help your students learn to choose a book for fun or interest that they can reasonably hope to read given their current reading skills.

My students sometimes wanted to read books that were quite challenging for them to read independently. Not wanting to cast doubt on their choices, I suggested that they could use the five-finger recommendation system to help decide if they could read it. Students read a test page to help them decide for themselves if a text will be too difficult. (If students chose a book about a topic of particular interest to them, they could always ignore using the five-finger recommendation.)

The Five-Finger Recommendation for Self-Selecting Books

1. Open the book to any page and begin reading.
2. Any time you come across a word that stumps you, hold up one finger.
3. If you are holding up five fingers before finishing a page, the book might be too hard for you to read on you own.

How to Start a Classroom Library

Keep in mind your goal. The quality and quantity of the books you have in the classroom library matter. You need enough books to have variety, but they should be the absolute best books you can find.

Get funding. Ask your administrator or school district for possible funds to get started.

Examine other teachers' setups. If any of your colleagues at your school or another school have classroom libraries, ask if you can visit. Or check out photos of classroom libraries on educational social media sites.

Seek book and magazine donations. Ask your students to help.

- Canvass *your students and their families* (grandparents, aunts, uncles, cousins) to donate magazines and books they might be ready to discard or take to a second-hand bookstore to sell. Students could canvass friends at extra-curricular activities and clubs.
- Ask the same of your *former students, friends* and *family members.*
- *Retiring teachers* are another good source. They may wish to donate their books to other teachers.
- Visit *local and second-hand bookstores.* They might be willing to donate or offer a discount on books for your classroom library.

Garage sales and flea markets might yield some gently used books for you and your students. I know many teachers who have entire series of books, such as Goosebumps, Magic School Bus, The Hunger Games, the Sisterhood of the Traveling Pants, His Dark Materials, and the Magic Tree House, which they found at garage sales when the children in the home had outgrown them and moved on as readers. You can be picky though. Build your library thinking "quality over quantity."

Subscribe to a bookselling group like Scholastic to receive books based on your students' book orders.

Invite local new and used bookstores to your classroom. Booksellers often love to visit schools and share new titles with teachers and their students. They often bring reading "bling" such as bookmarks, pins, and other freebies they receive from publishers to give away to students.

Teaching Tip

You might hit the jackpot at a garage sale. Be picky, though! Build your library thinking "quality over quantity."

Augment your library. You can boost your classroom library with public and school library books. You can sign these books out, usually for a month at a time, and then replace them with new titles. This strategy helps to keep enough turnover in titles so that students are exposed to new authors, books, genres, and formats on a regular basis. This maintains their interest in browsing your library. The school librarian is a great resource who will recommend reliably interesting books.

Label your personal books. You may wish to label the books you buy yourself with a stamp or by writing your name inside the cover. You will need to check on the school policy for books that you purchase using professional learning funds to find out if you can take these with you when you move from one school to another.

Your classroom library can begin as just one bookshelf full of interesting books.

Teaching Tip: *Seek Funding—It Works!*

When much of school literacy budgets are spent on program materials offered as a seeming panacea for weak reading scores, fewer resources are left to purchase books, magazines, and other reading material that would appeal to a wide variety of students. Valuable budget dollars end up being spent on materials that do not necessarily improve reading or the desire to read. Nonetheless, cultivating reading interest does not have to be at odds with helping students develop their reading skills. Make it a priority to have a conversation with the administrators and others planning the school budget to ensure you can get funding for reading resources that students can connect with and that make a difference in their lives.

In Cory's Classroom: Start with Your Interests

What do you like to read? Grade 7 social studies teacher Cory began his classroom library with books that interested him as a history major who was keenly interested in the world wars. He initially chose just a few books to have on a shelf in his classroom, such as *Generals Die in Bed* by Charles Yale Harrison, *Postcards from No Man's Land* by Aiden Chambers, and *War Horse* by Michael Morpurgo.

At the beginning of a class, Cory mentioned the books and said they were books he really enjoyed as a reader. A few students looked at the books when they finished their work and asked to take them to read. This is when Cory realized that having only a few books in his classroom was not going to meet the needs of his students. From there he began seeking out more and more titles, not only about the world wars but about anything to do with history and social studies. Within a few months, Cory had dozens of books and had created a display area at the back of the classroom for his developing classroom library.

Bolster the Reading Relationship with Action

New research tells us that comprehension might not be the last stop on the reading pathway. P. David Pearson and his colleagues say that "the job of comprehension is not complete until some significant action occurs—a story is told, a phenomenon is explained, an argument is constructed, a bias is unearthed and laid bare, a text is composed, or a product is created." (Peter Afflerbach, Gina Biancarosa, Matthew Hurt, & P. David Pearson, 2020, p. 236)

This link between comprehension and action is a new and exciting development for those who teach reading. To me, it means that reading comprehension inevitably leads me to do or feel something. I do not think that all reading must be followed by an action in the true sense of the word. If we remember that we read for knowledge, comfort, challenge, resonance, surprise, joy, reassurance, and, ultimately, discovery, then I would argue that reading comprehension is a relationship between reader and book that can *change* our lives and stay with us *all* our lives.

Response to a reading can take many forms. One of your students might pick up another book by Gene Luen Yang after enjoying *Boxers & Saints*. Another student might write a letter to a favorite author. Yet another might be more careful about recycling plastics after reading about environmental issues.

Think of a time that you took action based on something that you read. Did you initiate a conversation with a teaching colleague after reading a new book about literacy? Did you arrange a play date for your child after sharing a story together about friendship like *Stick and Stone* by Beth Ferry? Did you compose a tweet after reading a link to an article that interested you? Did you read another book? Did you simply register, in your mind, a new way of being human? All these actions were sparked by a book.

And these actions are evidence of a relationship with text. When students have this relationship—when a text has moved them, or changed them, or inspired them—they will likely come back to reading over and over again to experience that same connection. And when that transformation happens, that student has become a lifelong reader.

When a text has moved a child or changed them, or inspired them— they will come back to reading over and over again to experience that same connection.

In the Classroom: How Reading Can Spark Action Even in Kindergarteners

Let me tell you about what researcher Nigel Hall (1990) observed in a Kindergarten classroom when a group of five-year-old children were moved to act in response to a letter received at the school.

After having visited a local auto garage on a field trip, the children were planning to build a play-garage to be situated in a corner of their classroom. They would build it from discarded appliance boxes and other materials and be able to use it for play purposes once it was built.

The students were really excited about their garage project. Before they started construction, however, the teacher received a letter from a school neighbor. (It is my guess that the teacher did some behind-the-scenes work to encourage the writing and mailing of the letter, perhaps confiding in a neighborhood friend, family member, or retired teacher.)

Since the school year began, the students had been encouraged to read and write. Phonics was discussed but not overemphasized. In the letter, the teacher had the perfect opportunity to demonstrate an authentic purpose for reading! And so, the teacher showed the students the letter and together they read it aloud:

I have heard that you are going to build a garage. I wish to complain about it. Garages are very noisy, very dirty, and very dangerous. Someone may get hurt with all the cars. I do not think you should be allowed to build a garage.

The letter was discussed and debated at great length. The Kindergarten students were shocked by the letter's contents. They decided immediately to respond with personal letters of their own. Their letters were written using diagrams and their knowledge of phonics. Students read their letters aloud to each other and to the teacher. Hall noticed that some of the students' letters provided reassurance to the neighbor that they were being careful; others were persuasive about the importance of the garage; and a few suggested that the neighbor mind her own business. Ha!

Over several weeks, the students engaged in meaningful reading and writing activities that they were personally invested in as five-year-olds, all of which had been sparked by reading a letter. The good news is that the garage did get built and a final letter from the neighbor congratulated the students for taking into consideration her concerns. What a great example of how one letter can catapult a group of five-year-old students into action, into literacy, and into a relationship with the written word.

Your Key Takeaways

Here are the key ideas we explored in this chapter on inspiring a love of reading.

- Reading can and should be a lifelong pleasure.
- Picture books hold much potential for inspiring your students as readers. You can use them to explore with students a variety of important topics, themes, and areas of interest.
- Diverse literature creates opportunities for you to read aloud to provide your students with windows into others' realities, and mirrors to better understand themselves and their place in the world.
- Reading surveys are helpful to get the right books into the right hands because, for many readers, one book changes everything.
- Visiting school and public libraries helps to develop a life-long habit of reading.
- Classroom libraries warrant the time and effort to build them.
- Comprehension leads to action, and action is evidence of having a relationship with text. When that happens, students are on the pathway to becoming lifelong readers.

Conclusion: Where Does the Path Lead Now?

Reading is to the mind what exercise is to the body.
—*Joseph Addison, 1710*

If reading is exercise for the brain, *Sometimes Reading Is Hard* has been a rigorous workout. Likely, you have improved your understanding of how children learn to read. Perhaps you have enlarged your teaching toolbox with strategies to help you teach children to read.

Through the course of this book, we have removed the cognitive factors needed for reading—decoding, fluency, vocabulary, and comprehension—from their silos and shown how they can work with the motivational factors for reading—interest, choice, dedication, and collaboration. By using the cognitive and motivational factors for reading in combination, you can create the synergy that will help your students develop into the fluent, passionate, lifelong readers you know they can be.

In reading the pages of this book, you have taken in and absorbed a cornucopia of ideas, practices, strategies, research, resources, and classroom experiences. I hope these inspire you. I also hope that you have found a support group, of sorts, through the voices of the teachers and researchers presented in these pages.

Reading should not be presented to children as a chore, a duty. It should be offered as a gift.
—Kate DiCamillo

And now it is time to consider next steps. As we have seen, comprehension can lead to action. What action will you take, knowing what you now know about teaching reading? Of course, the actions you choose will depend on you and your students. You might make a personal commitment to build a classroom library or decide to read more children's books so you can find the absolute best books for your students. You might try a new vocabulary strategy or provide more time for explicit decoding instruction for that one student who hasn't mastered the sound-symbol relationship. Whatever action you decide to take, I wish you well.

Empowering a child with the skill of reading is, quite simply, an exceptional contribution to that child's life, inside and outside of school. Without dedicated teachers like you, many students simply would not learn to read. So, use your knowledge of the reading components to teach reading to your students every single day.

Why We Do It

I'd like to leave you with one final In the Classroom feature, from my own teaching experience. This is the story of Jessie, whom I taught in Grade 4. Jessie, more than any student I have taught, changed my thinking about teaching reading. Although I had no inkling of it at the time, Jessie was sending me on a quest to seek knowledge and understanding about those magical processes of reading and writing that changed my life. For Jessie and all our students, let's remember that every student has a way in. All we have to do is find those openings, and then find a way to respond. It can make all the difference.

In My Classroom: Jessie's Story

I was teaching Grade 4 and had a young student named Jessie in my class. Jessie seemed mostly uninterested in the reading and writing that we did for the first several months of the school year. I watched him engage in avoidance behaviors during reading and writing activities, especially when they were done individually.

One day, I asked my students to work in groups of three or four to reread a text from a book I had been reading aloud during class time and then to write a continuation of that story. Observing Jessie and two other students as they worked together, I noticed that something new was happening: Jessie was sharing his ideas with his peers and appeared engaged in the activity. This development made me hopeful that there were topics that interested him, and that I just needed to keep finding what those were to help him stay engaged in reading and writing.

As luck would have it, I did not have to wait long. A few days later, Jessie stayed back in the classroom after school. After everyone had left, he asked me if our class could have a pet show. A pet show! As a teacher, I had never hosted a pet show and wasn't even sure if we would be allowed to do this in our school. I was so pleased, however, that Jessie had suggested such an idea! I told him I would look into it and get back to him.

The next morning, I spoke to my principal and let him know what Jessie had asked for. I told him that I hoped to capture Jessie's interest and use this opportunity to help him develop his reading and writing skills by hosting the pet show. We got the go-ahead!

I began thinking of all the reading and writing that could be involved in having a pet show and became more and more excited about the prospect of hosting such an event. At the same time, I wondered about the wisdom of having a roomful of pets in the classroom. I put those thoughts aside, feeling that this was my opening: a way to involve Jessie in authentic reading and writing tasks about something Jessie himself had suggested.

Jessie was clearly excited. I put him in charge of the pet show, and we worked together to plan it out. We brainstormed the process we would follow as a class and had a daily check-in to talk about the plans. Jessie followed up each meeting with a to-do list for himself and for a few others who wanted to help.

Looking back, I realized that Jessie was involved in much more reading and writing than he had been before this. He researched how to host pets in the classroom. I helped him find articles about pets to read. He wrote letters, reread them, and revised them to send home to parents. Jessie surveyed the class to find out what kinds of pets his classmates would bring to school. And then he read about those pets so he would be prepared when they arrived.

We had our pet show, and it was a success. No one brought a snake, so I was happy! Overall, it was a learning experience unlike anything I had anticipated because the idea came from Jessie. His interest and passion for this project was the impetus for authentic reading, writing, and engagement. All I did was to notice, to advocate for him, and to create for him an opportunity to shine.

Acknowledgements

Sometimes reading is hard, but sometimes writing is hard too. But writing this book has been so worth it.

I wanted this book to be a resource for teachers like you. To help you in the incredible work you do teaching reading. But I also wanted to guard against telling you what to do. I have always believed that teachers are the best instructional decision makers in their classrooms. Writing in a way that honors this belief while conveying research-based and teacher-proven practices has been my goal throughout the writing process.

My former students have never been far from my thoughts. Neither have the many teachers, administrators, literacy coaches and consultants, and pre-service teachers I have had the honor to work with over the years. While writing, I drew on so many rich memories, some recent and some from the distant past. I would like to say to all of you, "If you ever doubt your efforts as a teacher, remember this: Your students never will."

I am grateful to the University of Lethbridge and the Faculty of Education for the gift of time for a study leave to research and write this book. I especially want to thank Dr. Sharon Pelech, Jaime Iwaasa, and Kelly Vaselenak for your incredible diligence in the faculty's Field Experience Office in my absence.

While I have wanted to write this book for some time, it would not have come about without the generous and kind support of Dr. Shelley Stagg Peterson, who introduced me to Mary Macchiusi at Pembroke Publishers. I would like to extend my sincere thanks to Shelley and to Mary, who asked me to articulate the reasons why I wanted to write "another book on reading." It was the perfect question. It helped me match my vision for this book with the right path for the teachers who would read it. My thanks also go to Margaret Hoogeveen, my editor, who provided insightful feedback and helped to make this book better. The result is a book unique to the lens of my own teaching experience and life as a teacher educator and researcher.

There are many special teachers in my life to thank, especially my first and most important teachers: my parents, Ed and Sheila Ryan, to whom I owe a huge debt of gratitude. While you are both missed more than I can express, your love of language and belief in me has made this journey possible.

Two classroom teachers made a significant difference in my life, my Grade 2 teacher, Mrs. Clarke, whose lesson about making toilet roll bunnies with only written instructions (no talking) will never be forgotten, and my band teacher for six years, Mr. Pokarney. You taught me that passion in learning must be nurtured by teachers who believe in the potential of their students.

My own children benefited from the wisdom and care of special teachers who made a remarkable difference in our lives. Mrs. Kathy Gill at Narnia Daycare, Mrs. MacDonald (who "taught Amy to read"), Mrs. Tory Neely-White, Mrs. Donna Dalby, Mr. Weatherall, and Dr. Sukalo, from Celebration High School in Florida. You saw, more than anyone, Amy's flair and passion for the written word. I cannot thank Mrs. Zahra Foroud, Mrs. Sandy Fraser, Mrs. Dawn King-Hunter, the late Lorraine Wolsey, and Mrs. Lola Major enough for being passionate about reading and learning, and for seeing the quiet strength, compassion, and humor of our youngest daughter, Erin. You provided the kind of support Amy and Erin needed to become passionate, lifelong readers.

Thank you to the many teachers I have called friends and colleagues throughout the years. I would like to especially acknowledge David Platt, Debbie Bingham, Lillian Snidal, Gaynel Day, Barb Yakabowski, Henny Hildebrand, Betty Bourassa, Mary Clamp, John Loree, Elton Tanne, and Pat Hales. Teaching was an absolute joy because of you.

Thank you also to my colleagues at the University of Victoria and the University of Lethbridge for your kind mentorship and friendship. I would like to thank particularly Dr. Allison Preece, Dr. Madge Craig, Dr. Peter Evans, Dr. Doug Petherbridge, Dr. Robert Anderson, Dr. Laurie Walker, Dr. Eric Mokosch, and especially Dr. Michael Pollard, Dr. Pamela Winsor, and Dr. Leah Fowler. I have always treasured talking with you about books and reading.

In working on this book, I could always count on my amazing teacher friends, to whom I could turn for insight, support, and meaningful conversations. Thank you, Rhona Harkness, Carol Young, Lucy Johnson, Jana Boschee, Marlin Howg, Deborah Yawney, Alisha Sims, and Cayley Ermter. Special thanks go to my amazing book gurus, Beth Cormier, Annette Bright, Kari Tanaka, and Becky Colbeck for always recommending the right books for any situation. Thank you, too, Margaret Beintema, for your amazing computer skills and, as always, your creative and practical solutions.

I would also like to thank the many pre-service teachers, near and far, whom I have had the pleasure of working with for almost 30 years. You taught me to keep believing in the power of teaching and learning for those young people in our classrooms. We may never get it perfect, but we will never stop trying.

Finally, to Glenn, for 40 years of believing in and supporting me. My love.

References

Adams, M. (1994). *Beginning to read: Thinking and learning about print*. New York, NY: Bradford Books.

Afflerbach, P., Biancarosa, G., Hurt, M., & Pearson, P.D. (2020). Teaching reading for understanding: Synthesis and reflections on the curriculum and instruction portfolio. In Pearson, P. D., Palinscar, A., Biancarosa, G., & Berman, A. (Eds.). *Reaping the rewards of the reading for understanding initiative* (pp. 215–247). Washington, DC: National Academy of Education.

Amato, J. (2021). *ProjectLit community*. Retrieved from https://www.facebook.com/projectlitcommunity/

Annan, K. (1997). United Nations International Literacy Day Secretary-General Message. Retrieved from https://www.un.org/press/en/1997/19970904.SGSM6316.html

Archer, A., Gleason, M., Vachon, V. (2003). Decoding and fluency: Foundation skills for struggling older readers. *Learning Disability Quarterly*. Retrieved from https://doi.org/10.2307/1593592

Aronson, M. (2014). Are teenagers reading less? Consider the source. *School Library Journal*, May. Retrieved from https://www.slj.com/?detailStory=are-teenagers-reading-less-consider-the-source

Atwell, N. (2007). *The reading zone*. New York, NY: Scholastic.

Atwell, N. (2014). *In the middle: A lifetime of learning about writing, reading, and adolescents* (3rd ed.). Portsmouth, NH: Heinemann.

Bauman, J., Ware, D., & Edwards, E. (2007). Bumping into spicy, tasty words that catch your tongue: A formative experiment on vocabulary instruction. *The Reading Teacher, Vol. 61* (2), 108–122.

Beck, I., McKeown, M., & Kucan, L. (2013). *Bringing words to life: Robust vocabulary* (2nd ed.). New York, NY: Guilford.

Beers, K. (2016). The whole-class novel: To read together or not? *Tyrolia*. Retrieved from http://kylenebeers.com/blog/2016/04/14/the-whole-class-novel-to-read-together-or-not/

Berthoud, E., & Elderkin, S. (2016). *The story cure: An a–z of books to keep kids happy, healthy, and wise*. Edinburgh: Canongate Books.

Bessette, H. (2020). Using choral reading to improve reading fluency of students with exceptionalities, *Georgia Journal of Literacy 43*(1), Article 8.

Bigozzi, L., Tarchi, C., Vagnoli, L., Valente, E., & Pinto, G. (2017). Reading fluency as a predictor of school outcomes across Grades 4–9. *Frontiers in Psychology*. Retrieved from doi:10.3389/fpsyg.2017.00200

Bishop, R. S. (1990). Mirrors, windows, and sliding glass doors. Keynote Address, *14th Annual Reading Conference Proceedings*, San Bernardino, California: CSUSB Reading Conference.

Brown, R. (2008). The road not yet taken: A transactional strategies approach to comprehension instruction. *The Reading Teacher, 61*(7), 538–547.

Cabell, S., Justice, L., McGinty, A., DeCoster, J., & Forston, L. (2015). Teacher-child conversations in preschool classrooms: Contributions to children's vocabulary development. *Early Childhood Research Quarterly, 30*(A), 80–92.

Clay, M. (2016). Literacy lessons designed for individuals. *International Electronic Journal of Elementary Education, 7*(1), 3–12.

Compton-Lilly, C., Mitra, A., Guay, M., & Spence, L. (2020). A confluence of complexity: Intersections among reading theory neuroscience, and observations of young readers. *Reading Research Quarterly*. Retrieved from https://doi.org/10.1002/rrq.348

Corcoran, C., & Davis, A. (2005). A study of the effects of readers' theater on second and third grade special education students' fluency growth. *Reading Improvement, 42*(2), 105+.

Cunningham, P., Hall, D., & Heggie, T. (2001). *Making words, grades 1–3.* New York, NY: Good Apple.

Cunningham, P., Hall, D., & Heggie, T. (2001). *Making big words, grades 3–6.* New York, NY: Good Apple.

Duke, N., & Pearson, P. (2008). Effective practices for developing reading comprehension. *The Journal of Education, 189*(1/2), 107–122.

Dweck, C. (2007). *Mindset: The psychology of success.* New York, NY: Ballantine Books.

Ebbers, S. (2004). *Vocabulary through morphemes: Suffixes, prefixes, and roots for intermediate grades.* Longmont, CO: Sopris West Educational Services.

Ebbers, S., & Denton, C. (2008). A root awakening: Vocabulary instruction for older students with reading difficulties. *Learning Disabilities Research & Practice, 23*(2), 90–102.

Education Review Office (2018). *Keeping children engaged and achieving in reading: Teaching approaches and strategies that work.* Wellington, NZ: New Zealand Government.

Fraumeni-McBride, J. (2017). The effects of choice on reading engagements and comprehension for second- and third-grade students: An action report. *Journal of Montessori Research, 3*(2), 19–38.

Frey, N. (2020). *The skill, will, and thrill of comprehension* [Video]. YouTube. https://www.youtube.com/watch?v=qwfyXO-VLZU

Gallagher, K. (2009). *Readicide: How schools are killing reading and what you can do.* Portsmouth, NH: Stenhouse.

Gambrell, L. (2015). Getting kids hooked on the reading habit. *The Reading Teacher,* Retrieved from https://doi.org/10.1002/trtr.1423

Gilgun, J. (n.d.). [Quote]. Retrieved from https://www.brainyquote.com/quotes/joe_gilgun_878821

Gladwell, M. (2011). *Outliers: Story of success.* New York: Hachette Book Group.

Graves, M., & Watts-Taffe, S. (2008). For the love of words: Fostering word consciousness in young readers. *The Reading Teacher, 62*(3), 185–193. Retreived from doi:10.1598/RT.62.3.1

Guthrie, J. (2013). Best practices for motivating students to read. In Morrow, L., & Gambrell, L. (Eds.). *Best Practices in Literacy Instruction* (5th ed.). New York: Guilford Press.

Hagerman, M. (2012, February 9). The simple view of online reading: It's time to push back. *Educational Technology.* Retrieved from https://mschirahagerman.wordpress.com/2012/02/09/the-simple-view-of-online-reading-its-time-to-push-back/

Hall, N. (1990). Real literacy in a school setting: Five-year-olds take on the world. *The Reading Teacher, 52*(1), 8–17.

Harmon, J., Wood, K., Hedrik, W., Vintinner, J., & Willeford, T. (2009). Interactive word walls: More than just reading the writing on the walls. *Journal of Adolescent & Adult Literacy, 52*(5), 398–408.

Hasan, N. (2014). Teaching vocabulary through collaboration: Students as independent readers, *Journal of Education and Practice, 5*(13), 60–68.

Hasbrouck, J. (2006). For students who are not yet fluent, silent reading is not the best use of classroom time. *American Educator, 30*(2). Retrieved from https://www.readingrockets.org/articles/researchbytopic/26224

Hattie, J. (2012). *Visible learning for teachers.* New York: Routledge.

Hibbert, K. (2002). Don't steal the struggle! The commercialization of literacy and its impact on teachers. *Education Publications, 34.* Retrieved from https://ir.lib.uwo.ca/edupub/34/

Hidi, S. (2001). Interest, reading, and learning: Theoretical and practical considerations. *Educational Psychology Review, 13*(3), 191–209.

Hoffman, J., Baumann, J., & Afflerback, P. (Eds.) (2014). *Elementary reading.* New York, NY: Routledge.

International Literacy Association (2018). Reading fluently does not mean reading fast. *Literacy Leadership Brief.* Retrieved from https://literacyworldwide.org/docs/default-source/where-we-stand/ila-reading-fluently-does-not-mean-reading-fast.pdf

Ivey, G., & Broaddus, K. (2001). "Just plain reading": A survey of what makes students want to read in middle school classrooms. *Reading Research Quarterly, 36*(4), 350–377.

Ivey, G., & Baker, M. (2004). Phonics instruction for older readers. Just say no. *Educational Leadership, 61*(6). Retrieved from http://www.ascd.org/publications/educational-leadership/mar04/vol61/num06/toc.aspx

Johnson, J. (2005). What makes a "good" reader? Asking students to define "good" readers. *The Reading Teacher, Vol. 58*(8), 766–770.

Juvonen, J. (2007). Reforming middle schools: Focus on continuity, social connectedness, and engagement. *Educational Psychologist, 42*(4), 197–208.

King, S. (2000). *On writing: A memoir of the craft (25th anniversary edition)*. New York, NY: Scribner.

LaBerge, D., & Samuels, S. (1974). Toward a theory of automatic information processing in reading. *Cognitive Psychology, 6*, 292–323.

Lesaux, N., Harris, J., & Sloan P. (2012). Adolescents' motivation in the context of an academic vocabulary intervention in urban middle school classrooms. *Journal of Adolescent & Adult Literacy, 56*(3), 231–240.

McKay, M. (2008). *Story vines and readers theatre: Getting started*. Winnipeg, MN: Portage & Main Press.

MacKenzie, T. (2019). How your teacher-librarian can be an ally when teaching with inquiry. *Mind Shift*. Retrieved from https://www.kqed.org/mindshift/53417/how-your-teacher-librarian-can-be-an-ally-when-teaching-with-inquiry

McCracken, M., & McCracken, R. (2012). *Spelling through phonics (30th anniversary edition)*. Winnipeg, MN: Portage & Main Press.

McGeown, S., Johnston, R., Walker, J., Howatson, K., Stockburn, A., & Dufton, P. (2015). The relationship between young children's enjoyment of learning to read, reading attitudes, confidence and attainment, *Educational Research, 57*(4), 389–402.

Mehigan, G. (2020). Effects of fluency-oriented instruction on motivation for reading of struggling readers. *Educational Science, 10*(3), 56.

Meyer, M. (1999). Repeated reading to enhance fluency: Old approaches and new directions. *Annals of Dyslexia, 49*, 283–306.

Miller, D. (2012). *Reading with meaning: Teaching comprehension in the primary grades*, (2nd ed.). Portsmouth, NH: Stenhouse Publishers.

Milner, J., & Milner, L. (1999). *Bridging English*. New York, NY: Pearson.

Muhammad, G. (2020). *Cultivating genius: An equity framework for culturally and historically responsive literacy*. New York, NY: Scholastic.

National Council of Teachers of English (2007). Statement on Classroom Libraries. Retrieved from https://ncte.org/statement/classroom-libraries/

Neuman, S. (2019). *Living in a world of words surrounded by book deserts*. [Video]. YouTube. https://www.youtube.com/watch?v=u32AfUfoJdw&feature=emb_logo

Neuman, S., & Dickinson, D. (2006). *Handbook of early literacy research, Vol. 2*. New York, NY: Guildford Press.

Oczkus, L. (2009). *Interactive think-aloud lessons: 25 surefire ways to engage students. And improve comprehension*. New York, NY: Scholastic Teaching Resources.

Oke, M. M. (2019). Rise in Canadian children's LGBTQ2+ literature offers more reflection and understanding. *Canadian Children's Book News, Winter*, 14–18.

Parrot, K. (2017). Fountas and Pinnell say librarians should guide readers by interest, not level. *School Library Journal*. Retrieved from https://www.slj.com/?detailStory=fountas-pinnell-say-librarians-guide-readers-interest-not-level

Pearson, P. D. (2020). *Fresh Ideas*. Learning to read: What really matters. 03/12. Retrieved from https://blog.savvas.com/learning-to-read-what-really-matters-with-dr-p-david-pearson/

Pearson, P. D., and Gallagher, M. (1983). The instruction of reading comprehension, *Contemporary Educational Psychology, 8*, 317–344.

Pearson, P. D., Palinscar, A., Biancarosa, G., & Berman, A. (Eds.). (2020). *Reaping the rewards of the reading for understanding initiative*. Washington, DC: National Academy of Education.

Ripp, P. (2017). *Passionate readers: The art of reaching and engaging every child*. New York, NY: Routledge.

Rog, L., & Burton, W. (2002). Matching texts and readers: Leveling early reading materials for assessment and instruction. *The Reading Teacher, 55*(4), 348–356.

Rosenblatt, L. (1978). *The reader, the text, the poem: The transactional theory of the literary work*. Carbondale: Southern Illinois University Press.

Routman, R. (2005). *Reading essentials: The specifics you need to teach reading well*. Portsmouth, NH: Heinemann.

Ruddel, M., & Shearer, A. (2002). Middle school at-risk students become avid word leaners with the vocabulary self-collection strategy (VSS). *Journal of Adolescent & Adult Literacy, 45*, 352–363.

Rupley, W., Logan, J., & Nichols, W. (1998/1999). Vocabulary instruction in a balanced reading program. *The Reading Teacher, 52*(4), 336–346.

Saaris, N. (2016). *From carrots to caring: Motivating students to read*. Actively Learn blog. Retrieved from https://www.activelylearn.com/post/from-carrots-to-caring-motivating-students-to-read

Sample, I. (2019). Blow to 10,000-hour rule as study finds practice doesn't always make perfect. *The Guardian*. Retrieved from https://www.theguardian.com/science/2019/aug/21/practice-does-not-always-make-perfect-violinists-10000-hour-rule

Sanden, S. (2014). Out of the shadow of SSR: Real teachers' classroom independent reading practices. *Language Arts, 91*(3), 161–175.

Save the Children (2013). *Kids from around the world tell us why they love to read.* Retrieved from https://savethechildren.typepad.com/blog/2013/02/kids-really-do-say-the-darndest-things-about-reading.html?msource =emeen30s0213

Scholastic Kids & Parents. (2017). *Kids and family report (7th Ed.)* . Retrieved from https://www.scholastic.com/readingreport/home.html

Swartz, L., & Peterson, S. S. (2015). *This is a great book! 101 events for building enthusiastic readers inside and outside the classroom—from chapter books to young adult novels.* Markham, ON: Pembroke Publishers.

Shanahan, T. (2020). What constitutes a science of reading? *Reading Research Quarterly, 55* (S1). Retrieved from https://doi.org/10.1002/rrq.349

Springer, S., Harris, S., & Dole, J. (2017). From surviving to thriving: Four research-based principles to build students' reading interest. *The Reading Teacher, 71*(1), 43–50.

Stanovich, K. (1986). Matthew effects in reading: Some consequences of individual differences in the acquisition of literacy, *Reading Research Quarterly, (21)* 4, 360–406.

Stern, S. (2014). View from the chalkboard: Fun Fridays with tongue twisters support fluency in the Reading Room. *The Reading Teacher. Vol. 68*(3), 189.

Tanaka, K. [@KariTanaka] (November 12, 2020). You know what the best book of the year was? The 1 that a child stayed up all night to read. The 1 that a striving reader stuck with until the very end. The 1 that made a child ask for a sequel. The 1 that a child saw themself in. If your book was loved by 1, it's the best book! [Tweet]. Twitter. Retrieved from https://twitter.com/KariTanaka/status/1327046932032675840

Tatum, A. [@AlfredTatum] (September 17, 2017). Leveled texts lead to leveled lives. [Tweet]. Twitter. Retrieved from https://twitter.com/AlfredTatum/status/909563807525216256

Tovani, C. (2020). *Why do I have to read this? Literacy strategies to engage our most reluctant students.* Portsmouth, NH: Stenhouse Publishers.

Trelease, J., & Giorgis, C. (2019). *Jim Trelease's read-aloud handbook (8th ed.)* . New York, NY: Penguin Books.

Tyerman, M., BonBernard, T., & Cardinal, P. (2006). *Our Alberta: Book 1.* Toronto: Nelson.

Vygotsky, L. S. (1978). *Mind in society: The development of higher psychological processes.* Cambridge, MA: Harvard University Press.

Wasik, B. (2001). Phonemic awareness and young children. *Childhood Education, 77*(3), 128.

Watt, T. S. (1954). Brush up your English. In Taylor, I., and Taylor, M. M. (1983). *The Psychology of Reading.* New York: Academic Press, 99.

Wigfield, A., Gladstone, J., & Turci, L. (2016). Beyond cognition: Reading motivation and reading comprehension. *Child Development Perspectives.* Retrieved from doi:10.10.1111/cdep.12184.

Wilfong, L. (2008). Building fluency, word-recognition ability, and confidence in struggling readers: The poetry academy. *The Reading Teacher, 62*(1), 4–13.

Wolf, M. (2018). *Reader, come home.* New York, NY: HarperCollins Publishers.

Wolf, M. (2000). *Proust and the squid.* New York, NY: HarperCollins Publishing.

Index